SOME OF THE DEAD
ARE STILL BREATHING

Also by Charles Bowden

Killing the Hidden Waters (1977)

Street Signs Chicago: Neighborhood and Other Illusions of Big-City Life, with Lewis Kreinberg and Richard Younker (1981)

Blue Desert (1986)

Frog Mountain Blues, with Jack W. Dykinga (1987)

Trust Me: Charles Keating and the Missing Billions, with Michael Binstein (1988)

Mezcal (1988)

Red Line (1989)

Desierto: Memories of the Future (1991)

The Sonoran Desert, with Jack W. Dykinga (1992)

The Secret Forest, with Jack W. Dykinga and Paul S. Martin (1993)

Seasons of the Coyote: The Legend and Lore of an American Icon, with Philip L. Harrison (1994)

Blood Orchid: An Unnatural History of America (1995)

Chihuahua: Pictures from the Edge, with Virgil Hancock (1996)

Stone Canyons of the Colorado Plateau, with Jack W. Dykinga (1996)

Juárez: The Laboratory of Our Future, with Noam Chomsky and Eduardo Galeano (1998)

Eugene Richards, with Eugene Richards (2001)

Down by the River: Drugs, Money, Murder, and Family (2002)

Blues for Cannibals: The Notes from Underground (2002)

A Shadow in the City: Confessions of an Undercover Drug Warrior (2005)

Inferno, with Michael P. Berman (2006)

Exodus/Éxodo, with Julián Cardona (2008)

Trinity, with Michael P. Berman (2009)

Murder City: Ciudad Juárez and the Global Economy's New Killing Fields (2010)

Dreamland: The Way Out of Juárez, with Alice Leora Briggs (2010)

The Charles Bowden Reader (2010)

El Sicario: The Autobiography of a Mexican Assassin, with Molly Molloy (2011)

The Red Caddy: Into the Unknown with Edward Abbey (2018)

SOME OF THE DEAD ARE STILL BREATHING

LIVING IN THE FUTURE

Charles Bowden

FOREWORD BY SCOTT CARRIER

University of Texas Press
Austin

Lannan
CHARLES BOWDEN PUBLISHING PROJECT

Requests for permission to reproduce material from this work should
be sent to:
Permissions
University of Texas Press
P.O. Box 7819
Austin, TX 78713-7819
utpress.utexas.edu/rp-form

⊗ The paper used in this book meets the minimum requirements of
ANSI/NISO Z39.48-1992 (R1997) (Permanence of Paper).

Library of Congress Cataloging-in-Publication Data

Names: Bowden, Charles, 1945-2014, author.
Title: Some of the dead are still breathing : living in the future /
Charles Bowden.
Description: Austin : University of Texas Press, 2018. | "The first
edition of *Some of the Dead Are Still Breathing* was published in
2009 by Houghton Mifflin Harcourt."
Identifiers: LCCN 2017050183
  ISBN 978-1-4773-1690-0 (pbk. : alk. paper)
  ISBN 978-1-4773-1691-7 (library e-book)
  ISBN 978-1-4773-1692-4 (non-library e-book)
Subjects: LCSH: Bowden, Charles, 1945-2014—Travel—Southwest, New.
| Bowden, Charles, 1945-2014—Travel. | Bowden, Charles, 1945-2014—
Prophecies. | Southwest, New—Description and travel. | Voyages and
travels. | Natural history. | Ecology. | Social change. | Social
prediction.
Classification: LCC F787 .B695 2018 | DDC 917.7904—dc23
LC record available at https://lccn.loc.gov/2017050183

doi:10.7560/316900

All my means are sane,
my motive and object mad.

CAPTAIN AHAB

Every moving thing that liveth shall
be meat for you; even as the green herb
have I given you all things. But flesh
with life thereof, which is the blood
thereof, shall ye not eat.

GENESIS 9:3–4

Contents

Foreword

SCOTT CARRIER

I should start with a forewarning for those readers who wish to feel safe—put this book down and walk away now. Reading Charles Bowden is like climbing a steep mountain at night, alone, with the trail disappearing behind you. He lures you along with clear beautiful sentences.

Fireflies, floating, like the glow off the cigarettes as the men sit in the growing dark of the farmyard with their bottles and loves and tears.

And then you realize you've followed him to the edge of a cliff.

We can't wrap our minds around the vast dying now taking place. . . . We cannot say this thing about people, that there are too many of us and not enough of everything else.

You can't turn back because you know what he's saying is true. There is no going back. The future is already here and it's scary as hell. So what can be done, what move do you make? How do you live a moral life in a culture of death?

If you don't want to go there, if trembling is not your cup of tea, just put the book down now and write Bowden off with your favorite curse or slander.

For those of you who wish to continue, there are some things you should know before you go.

Bowden's plan from the beginning of his career was to write the real history of his time on earth. He wanted to create an endless work like Dickens did with his novels, only he was going to do it in nonfiction—real people, real lives—in the American Southwest.

He didn't intend to get sucked into a human catastrophe with drugs, violence, murder, mayhem. In the 1980s and 1990s the drug trade and illegal immigration exploded along the U.S.-Mexico border, on his turf, on his watch, and he felt a moral obligation as a writer to tell people what was going on and why. He spent thirty years in an undeclared war zone covering real-life horror stories like mothers carrying their babies across the desert, crossing the border, and dying from dehydration on U.S. soil or the torture/murders in Juárez where bodies were cut up and the parts rearranged as conceptual art for public display. Sometimes his editors sat on stories for months or a year because they didn't believe they were true.

But the stories were true and were eventually published in magazines such as *Harper's*, *Mother Jones*, *Esquire*, and *GQ*, and in books that Chuck wrote without a contract so he wouldn't have to describe what he was working on. He wrote it all down to show people what was happening, and people didn't care. Things didn't get better, they got worse—more mothers carrying their babies across the border and dropping from dehydration on U.S. soil, more murders in Juárez with bodies cut up and the parts rearranged as conceptual art to put on public display. By the time Chuck wrote this book he'd given up hope that his work or anybody's work was going to slow the rate of carnage.

This work took a toll on Chuck's physical and mental health, especially the way he did it. His method of reporting, the way he figured out what happened and why, was to become the people he was writing about. He would enter their minds and bodies to see and feel the world as they did. This sounds impossible but it's what hunters have done for hundreds of thousands of years, enter the mind of their prey.

He would become them, and once he did that, he would understand why the thing happened, why they behaved that way, why they lied, why they told the truth, why they are who they are. He once befriended and entered the mind of a man who had personally tortured and killed 250 people, boiled them alive in some instances. He wrote the story and sent it to *Harper's*, but he didn't forget what he'd learned or what he'd seen. Bowden thought forgetting was a sin.

So he tried to write in a way that you couldn't forget. He wrote in a way that was rational and also irrational, logical and emotional, back and forth, like the way we exist as animals. He said he couldn't write unless he thought it was music, that way he beat back his own cowardice. And he believed deeply that American writing was about rhythm. He had a rap about how American literature started with Lincoln's second inaugural address because it's written with the rhythm and emotional pacing of a black Christian sermon.

On the occasion corresponding to this four years ago all thoughts were anxiously directed to an impending civil war. All dreaded it, all sought to avert it. While the inaugural address was being delivered from this place, devoted altogether to saving *the Union without war, insurgent agents were in the city seeking to* destroy *it without war—seeking to dissolve the Union and divide effects by negotiation. Both parties deprecated war, but one of them would* make *war rather than let the nation survive, and the other would* accept *war rather than let it perish, and the war came.*

"And the war came" is a drum beat, an upbeat anticipating a downbeat, propelling sound and energy forward. According to Bowden, this energy, this rhythm, originates in the ground. It comes up from underground, and it's different in different places, different times, and different cultures that are there to feel it. In this case it was coming from the Mississippi Delta during slavery and it was so strong, so emotionally powerful that it infected the minds of writers in other parts of the country. The focus on the natural rhythms of speech coming up from the ground, you can feel it in Twain, Steinbeck, Faulkner, Hemingway. These writers make us feel the landscape through the rhythm of speech.

Do you follow?

Think of it this way. Before Bowden would start writing he had to come to ground. "I got to come to ground." He'd say it like there didn't need to be any more explanation. I pictured him lying face down on the desert floor, fingers squeezing the sand. But I don't think he did that. I think it was more like what his girlfriend Beulah the rattlesnake taught him— sit quietly and go into snake time. Feel the beat, the flowing energy underground. The ancient Greeks called it the Chthonic and they had priests with snakes, Pythonists, who could see the future.

When Bowden came to ground he sang the blues, the Sonoran blues.

Here the land always makes promises of aching beauty, and the people always fail the land. (Blue Desert)

So don't be expecting this book to have a happy ending, and don't be expecting it to make sense. You will feel lost, the world slipping away and weeping mothers. Then demons will come. And here's where we learn what the song is all about: Don't turn away. Don't turn away from the demons, they decide if they stay or go. Don't turn away from the demons, say yes instead of no.

I think he would forgive me that rhyme, but that's not the way he'd put it.

He'd put it as what follows, a redemption song of sorts. I once asked Chuck if he was religious and he said no, not at all. That he wasn't a Christian and didn't have the energy to be an atheist because then you have to get out of bed and have arguments about whether God exists.

"Who gives a shit?" he said. "God doesn't."

So I don't think he was concerned about being redeemed from sin and evil. He wasn't looking to be saved in the blood of the lamb. Bowden's redemption comes through the eye of an elephant or a snake or a tree. And if that's not enough then maybe you are dead but still breathing.

SOME OF THE DEAD
ARE STILL BREATHING

Floating

*Golden light pours on the scrubbed wood floor in the kitchen
by the woodstove as they bend over the chair driving brass
tacks to hold down the green fabric on the seat in the August
of a summer, and out the window, wood sash and glass framed
in small squares, out there the sky is blue and oaks brush the
horizon, a green fur of the leaves, soon dusk will come and
the fireflies but now the tap tap tap of the small upholster-
ing hammer, a wood handle and brass head, my father with
a hand-rolled cigarette in his mouth, my mother fussing to
keep the fabric smooth, and near at hand a brass ashtray cut
from the fired end of a cannon shell from far away, out there
on the oceans of the world during the last war, the one before
the next war, and I can hear men in the house, all young men
in blue starched uniforms and with bibs and white sailor
hats and they drink from quart bottles and smoke short
strong cigarettes and smile at me as I toddle around, and
they don't know what to do with themselves because they are
still alive and when they drain those quart bottles day after day and week after week the others come back and stare,
and this comforts them and frightens them and so they drink
and drink and my mother can barely stand this, cooking for
a mob, the men drunk in the morning and the night, and
my father hears her out but does nothing because he knows*

even though he will not say this knowing, knows that this must continue until it ends, that there is a blood price to be paid and so his huge stone farmhouse, fourteen rooms plus outbuildings, teems with the living who drink with the dead.

Maybe it never begins but if it does begin, I think it begins at that moment, the world of green and blue pouring through the century-old glass, the tap of the hammer, the pies cooling on the counter, the low smoky comfort of the woodstove that never grows cool, the men broken but held together by bottles, the ocean whispering from the sawed-off cannon shells, the fabric of life unraveling before me and yet caressing my face.

That is the floor of my optimism, all from a room and afternoon and time that was vanishing as fast as I swallowed it, a war fading, the sun sinking, the pies cooling, the woodstove soon to be replaced by gas, the pump in the yard to become a pipe to a faucet, the privy to be abandoned, the farm to be fled, the roar of the city to fill my ears, the sky above to fill day by day with airplanes screaming, and the fields and the creek and the rank growth and rich earth to move away from me and yet always stay near, as close as fireflies floating in the last moments of a summer dusk.

There is blood also, constant killing of beasts for the table. Constant small words about the dead and the fear and the dread of dying any instant.

And song.

I want to wear that crown of glory,
When I get home to that good land;
Well I want to shout salvation's story,
In concert with ohh the blood-washed band.

That is how it begins for me and I have never envied other beginnings.

Because everything was in place in my beginning, there was no other, no rupture, no evil, no innocence.

Fireflies, floating, like the glow off the cigarettes as the men sit in the growing dark of the farmyard with their bottles and loves and tears.

Red

I see red. The color flashes across the gray light as the black coffee wafts across my face. The dark comforts me and so I rise before first light. The moonless nights are best because in the blackness even the trees lack form. Shapes slowly enter the yard, the stone body of Saint Francis, big clump of vine stroking the mesquite. Everything gray at first. The first licks of color—a tint of green, a blush of rose—come and go. I have read for years about photons of light and the structure of our eyes and how our cells and structure in the eyes form colors. Other species see a different world.

I understand none of this. Since I waddled in diapers, I have marveled at color creeping into the land at gray light and then slowly drenching everything in my gaze.

At gray light, I always believe but I cannot clearly tell myself what this belief is. But with that first cup of coffee, I am always a yes man. And this feeling can continue past the midnight hour.

Names don't help me much anymore. They belong to that time when everything was kept in its place. Before the winds came up and the water came up and licked the land away, this land is your land, this land is my land, this land is gone.

For more than fifty years I have come to this place, a city older than our flag, and now it is dead. Nine months ago I was in the dead city after the wind rose, the levees breached, and water came in. Two months ago I was again in the dead city. Soon, I know I must return to the dead city.

I sat in the Napoleon House, a bar in the quarter where Sherwood Anderson and William Faulkner hashed out the future of American literature in the 1920s. Two blocks away, Tennessee Williams wrote the play. I ate red beans and rice, had a glass of wine. I walked through the open door of a house, studied the splotches of mold on the wall, and felt the sadness on the abandoned pool table covered with the gray powder left by the waters. An overhanging stained glass lamp stared at the felt with a dead eye.

A few days ago I was out in the desert with the dead trees and empty skies. I stood by an ironwood, a species good for seven or eight hundred years. The small tree seemed more dead than alive, a mound of spent limbs with a few struggling leaves here and there. I stooped and examined a cascade of earlier struggles, ledges in the stump where the plant had all but died, then rallied when caressed by a breath of rain and shot up a new stem which thickened and in, say, two hundred years' time also faced that killing drought, died back and then this plateau of doom lifted and yet another new stem raced to drink the sun and believe once again in immortality.

Before that I was in a city of the south, past the snake of dirt linking two continents, in that south of the Americas, the place celebrating another pain, climbing hillsides where residents clamber up slopes equal to a twenty-five-story building to reach their homes. I got out of a car with a local and he told me to take off my jacket, a beat-up blue windbreaker with twenty years of abuse. He said it was too bright. In the clinic up on the hillside, the two women helping with the various local ailments offered that drug use and pregnant twelve-year-olds were high on the list of local medical problems.

"How tough is it here?" I asked.

One woman looked at my old tennis shoes and explained that I could be killed for such footgear. She was forty-seven years old and had lived here all of her life.

"What do you do about the gangs?" I asked.

"I avoid their eyes," she said as her eyes met mine.

At the street markets in the city center, bras and panties, all the stalls illegal, everyone looks and no one seems to buy. At night the streets go cold, everything shuts down, and men sprawl on the sidewalks with foil pipes smoking *basuco*, the potion rendered from cocaine paste, and young men stare with hungry eyes and women in short skirts with breasts spilling out look with greedy eyes and night comes down like the lid on a garbage can and I have no answer and would believe no answer given me and I think of the dead city back home where the hurricane came and then the big water and the abandoned houses with one word spray-painted on some lonely and ruined homes, BAGHDAD.

One day when gray clouds rolled in I sat in the low light and wanted the words and metaphors to be over. Maybe someone can write a scene like this: we are all on a train and it is racing toward a bridge that is out but no one on the train cares because they are busy arguing about train security measures or who gets to sit in which car or whether the train is only for people or whether the train is only for one sex or the other or maybe the train should be divided up according to race or language or religion and still the train races toward the bridge that is gone, races toward some chasm that will shatter it and so the people argue and do not care that their behavior means they can never reach the future.

But words are all I have, my skills are limited and the words at best are a veil, maybe even a shroud, between us and this world we touch but cannot embrace, a ball of dirt we stand on but never can really know. We want a clean thing, we want ten commandments, a list of solid answers, a form we fill out and then we're done with the mysteries, perhaps, a chant we can murmur in the dark hours. But the real writing is not on any page, it is everywhere. Cities have morphed into giant splatters of flesh and materials and we call them mega this and that but our words cannot capture the reality that slaps our faces. We can't wrap our minds around the vast dying now taking place, the exit of plants and animals without even a goodbye note as they leave us behind, and it is not like the near-beer version peddled by the Good Book merchants of gloom, no, it is the silence of life fleeing this place of life, the silent caravan of beasts and fish in the sea and whales leaving our world and going over Jordan, but this time the land is not promised but forsaken. People, we can't talk about people, people everywhere, crowding the beaches, jamming their lives into the canyons, smearing the plains with their houses and ribbons and bows, terracing hillsides with shacks that barely get them through the lonely nights. We cannot say this thing about people, that there are too many of us and not enough of everything else.

And so we turn away and dream of the warm soft times, when lullabies caressed our faces and we bathed in the twinkle of the stars on those first summer nights. We have ceased to say things. Soon, as more cities go dead, we will struggle to remember their names. Just as the vanishing beasts are nowhere on our tongues.

I am driving down a back road and find a tortoise sitting on the asphalt. I stop and move it to the ditch and it clambers off into the tall grass. Living in the future, both of us.

They are a family of three, the male a brilliant red, the female drab gray with rivulets of scarlet, and fledgling blotches of red and gray and the dark beak of an immature. They always come early to the feeders to avoid the din of the hundreds of birds that will soon descend. The old metal chair creaks as I lean forward to watch them. The pair nested this spring in the oleanders on the east side of the house, a fact I knew as a kind of rumor. Cardinals are easy to spot and yet furtive by nature and tend to live in a band of life that runs three to eight feet off the ground. The ground here whispers life. My best friend's ashes nourish a cactus three feet from my coffee cup. Those last few months, when he was drowning in a cocktail of suicide, drink, electroshock, cocaine, detox, and games of chance, he'd sit on the patio with glazed eyes, and birds would sing in the yard and bounce from limb to limb. I was never sure he noticed.

On the hillsides outside of my town, palo verdes stand dead, with their scant leaves and green skin, their skeletal limbs scratching the dry blue sky. The rains have failed for more than a decade and now trees native to this ground begin to die.

The cardinals flash past my eyes and the female disappears into a grove of pachypodium palms, a succulent from Africa. When we planted them a friend steeped in horticulture told us they would at best last three to five years and then would come a killing frost. For some seasons, we covered them with blankets in the winter. By the time they grew too tall for such efforts, the earth had begun to warm and the freezes had stopped and they flourish.

The male cardinal is up in the mesquite over the palms, the fledgling off to one side with a look almost of abandonment. Cardinals raise from two to four broods a season, and the fledgling is about to get the boot. *Cardinalis cardinalis* is territorial, like a lot of bird species. Male robins will attack a stuffed robin if the chest booms a decent red but ignore a stuffed immature robin with its dull feathers. You can see a war out there, or you can see a friendly place. Or you can simply see and skip the words.

Our feeders swallow 150 pounds of seed a month, birds have thronged here during all my good times and bad times.

They know my face and fall from the sky when they see me put out food in the first light of day. When storms whip through the desert, strange species descend, refugees from the winds. Sometimes pelicans from the distant Gulf of California arrive with shell-shocked eyes and must be trucked back to a realm of water and fish.

The female cardinal alights on the top of a trellis with the dry spine of a palo verde stem in her mouth. She swoops and again disappears into the palms. She is building a nest. In the nation of cardinals, the females are the builders.

The cardinals now number a hundred million. A century ago, they were a southern songbird. Now they are in Canada. They have caught a favoring wind.

Not so long ago, borders were lines on a map hardly noticed on the actual ground. Years ago I sat on a sand dune while a family from Oaxaca—a man, the wife in her long Indian skirt, and two toddlers—huddled under a creosote bush fifteen feet away, alert. We were all maybe twenty feet south of the line, two Border Patrol trucks staring at us. The Oaxacans were waiting for the trucks to move on so that they could dart into the nation to the north. The day was hot, the air dry. The fence was a sketch of wire running feeble under the huge blue sky. Other Mexicans lived all over the dunes in huts made of loading dock pallets and cardboard.

I thought if the poor were streaming up in family-size chunks from the distant south, then the earth itself was failing. I could not find a name for this new condition. Now everywhere is a line and crossing these lines grows harder and the lines themselves leap magically upward and become walls and razor wire and bullets and cells, absolute.

The cardinals come and go all day, the red slicing my eye. The heat is rising on my ground, the rains vanishing, and still they build that nest as I sit with coffee by the ashes of a defeated friend.

In 1886, cardinals were rarely sighted north of the Ohio River. By 1895, they were living around the Great Lakes. They moved into Iowa, then the Dakotas, following the Missouri River and its tributaries. They colonized southern Canada. The move north seemed to follow people, their yards and their feeders. And all this began to happen before temperatures seemed to rise and rise.

In the city of the south, revolution is in the mouth of the government but is not the sound of the streets. The market is car horns, constant car horns, car alarms rapping in the background, voices shouting and laughing, the roar of cycles, buses grinding through the gears, the rings and chirps of cell phones, the swish of awesomely tight jeans, music blaring from boom boxes, always hip-hop and always with a drum machine, a walloping sound that never ends and shrieks and squeals and roars and thumps and slides and crashes, a pounding on the skull that functions like smog in the great cities of the earth: so omnipresent it is all but undetectable. The standard uniform is tight britches and halter tops and generous breasts shored up by ferocious brassieres. The nation is the vanity center of the Western Hemisphere, famed for its beauty queens, a champ in per capita expenditure on cosmetics. The going rate for a new chest is about twenty-two dollars a month. The women here walk with a slight sway to the hips, and they carry their breasts before them like sliced melons on a tray. It is the only nation I have visited where I have been fortunate enough to observe them stashing cell phones in their cleavage. The mannequins in the market all face ass-outward, the buttocks like kettledrums.

The traffic crawls. One day, I time the progress of a car length at ninety seconds. Another day, three feet in one minute. The drivers are creative, storming down one-way streets against traffic, changing lanes with a faith in God that far exceeds my own.

It hardly matters where this place is because it is so many places now. The spices vary, the weather also. But it is a city and it keeps growing and there is no work and no one really believes there will be work. They just live here after a fashion.

There are programs, policies, plans, meetings, slogans, marches, and lots of things to drink out of bottles. The revolution has arrived here and its color is red.

I get out of my chair, walk to the palms. In the fork of the tree, where small arms reach out to support four crowns of leaves, I can see the nest.

I drink their belief like a drug.

A guy I know told me, "History's been carjacked."

He said his friends thought he was bipolar.

My beliefs are dull and dismissed out of hand.

I believe that resources are limited and that no existing or imagined energy system can sidestep this fact.

I believe that the increase in human numbers inhales ever more resources.

I believe no energy system will deliver the punch of our declining fossil fuels at the same price.

I believe no energy system will solve our problems since the problems come from within us and not from our turbines.

I believe in red wine. And the scent of women. And the nuzzle of all dogs of all ages.

I believe political systems create no resources but devour them at varying rates.

I believe the politics of the right and left matter not at all to the bird on the wing or the trees dying on the hillsides.

I believe in the future because the future is here and I am in it.

I believe. Not wonder. Not doubt. Not know. I believe.

I believe in the dead city. I believe in the nest.

I also believe in the late quartets of Beethoven and Gershwin's "Summertime."

Oh, my God, do I believe.

A curved-bill thrasher, an aggressive bird, alights on the spiny trunk of the palm and moves up toward the nest. The male cardinal falls from the sky and assaults the thrasher, who flees with a stunned look in its eyes.

The titmouse, a tiny species, nests in holes in trees. Should another bird or a man or other beast peer in, the titmouse weaves its head and hisses exactly like a snake. This behavior is called mimicry. Sometimes, I call it love. Sometimes, I think it is simply the word *yes*.

Around here, they say it is time to get clean. Colonel Sanders is sad and has a banner saying so, draped across the front of KFC. The hundred stalls lining Poppy Lane stare out like broken teeth, without a single customer. Near the hole in the ground, Polo and Versace soldier on, as does a nearby McDonald's. A sign in one store advises WE ♥ BALI! START AGAIN. At the nearby Time Zone, a huge video arcade, the uniformed staff play the machines—there are no customers. They stare into the screens and kill various enemies with automatic weapons. The Time Zone banner rattles on about "the horrible tragedy on October 12 has only given us the deepest sorrow and the anxiety. Always be aware and take a prayer is the only way to avoid the same tragedy." The police man a table with a list of the dead and a collection bowl seeking money for the injured. The tablecloth drapes to the ground and someone has spray-painted on the fabric, FUCK

TERRORISTS. The air sags with humidity and with incense from the countless *canangs*—little trays with burning sticks of scent, flower petals, and some food, a bit of bread, a cookie—all to beckon the Hindu gods.

An Aussie talks softly, everyone here speaks very softly. He is telling me of four girls who were sitting over there, where the sun beats down on a bare wall across the rubble. The Sari Club—an open bar area with a cluster of thatched roofs—was full, he explains, and one of the four girls went to the bathroom while the other three stayed at the table. He pauses, his face beaded with sweat, his shirtless chest red from the sun. The bathroom is more or less intact, only a door and one wall blown away. Toward the back of the club, a tower of Coca-Cola crates remains—the full glass bottles gleaming, the red plastic cases a molten mass flowing downward.

On the evening of October 12, 2002, at Kuta Beach in Bali, three bombs went off in a fifty-five-second span and killed close to two hundred people and injured around five hundred. The first one went off in Paddy's Club, a two-story structure that now lacks a roof but still hosts a mezzanine of charred cocktail tables and a gutted ground floor. People fled out into the street. The second bomb exploded in a van parked in front of the Sari Club, catty-corner to Paddy's, a legendary watering hole full of hot young flesh, almost all of it Australian, European, and American (Balinese were banned, to cut down on hustling by prostitutes). The van left a hole about twelve feet across and several feet deep that gouges into what was once the street. A third blast went off near the U.S. consulate.

Parents flooded in from Australia looking for their children. And the children fled Bali, looking for bars without bombs. The damage ran to 17 cars, 450 buildings (17 completely destroyed), and a price tag of 3.5 billion Rupiah. An estimated three million Indonesians were forced into poverty as a result of the collapse of tourism.

The Balinese of Kuta Beach are baffled still. Bali is a Hindu island in the Muslim sea of Indonesia. In the late sixties, young backpackers with hungers and small change discovered Bali and strung it on the trail that linked Goa and Katmandu and Bangkok as stations of some new friendly cross. By the end of the millennium, maybe ten thousand people were arriving each day for the beaches and the clubs. Huge hotels erupted out of the little peninsula and tourists became the Balinese economy. Now arrivals are down to a thousand or fifteen hundred. The sole industry has collapsed—hotel occupancy, if they are open, is running in the single digits.

For the moment, it is about getting clean. The Balinese insist the rubble be dumped at sea. The rubble is dirty, they believe, because it is commingled with the residue of people who died violently. Piles of floral wreaths heap against the ruins. Hindu holy squads in silken sarongs come regularly to pray for the dead, to beg them to leave and go in peace. On Halloween weekend, the government in Jakarta flew in a thousand celebrities to brighten Kuta and prove it was back to normal.

One government official from Jakarta asked me, "Why don't tourists come?"

I said, "People don't like to have a drink and a bomb at the same time." He looked almost hurt.

The Aussie has fallen silent, his lips a thin line. He stares at the rubble where the four women sat. A few pieces of iron maybe thirty feet high have been propped up in a conscious echo of the surviving girders at the World Trade Center. The few tourists here all refer to the sight as Ground Zero, a new kind of landfall for modern voyeurs.

At a wine bar, I am the only customer. The Balinese bartender makes about forty bucks a month, plus a bonus if business is good. Business is no longer good. He's got a room, a wife, a daughter, motorcycle, television, refrigerator, and CD player. When the first bomb went off, he thought his propane tank had blown. Then people came running past shouting, "Bomb! Bomb!" Two days later, he went to the hospital and saw the corpses.

"I not stay long there," he continues. "I can't see, I can't see. A corpse, all burned without hands. Oh, God. I can't see."

In the weeks after the blast, friends who live near the bomb site heard screams in the night. Ceremonies have to be done, he says, so that the dead will leave.

One of the dead left early. Isabel von Jordan, a twenty-four-year-old German, danced in the Sari Club an hour before the detonation. After, she flew to Australia to visit friends wounded in the blast. On October 22, she took a swim in Kakadu National Park, where a four-meter crocodile killed her.

Priests throughout Bali recommended a mass cremation for the dead, and hotel management supported this decision. The local paper opines that "the hectic appeal of materialism offered by the tourism business has made many activists ignore the laws stipulated by God Almighty." For the cleansing, a *Bhuta Yadnya* rite was called for in two forms: the *pengulapan* or *mecaru,* asking that the dead not succumb to bad powers, and the *guru paduka,* asking forgiveness for the sins of the Balinese people.

The Aussie never really finishes his story. He squints in the afternoon sun and stares at the broken concrete, twisted beams, gutted cars, and small chunks of what was party time. He arrived three days after the bombing anyway, and the story is just something he heard. He drifts off, his voice fading like a dying radio.

After about a week—I'm careless with such records—the nest is finished. It's not much to look at, a cone maybe three or four inches high and five or six across. I do not measure it because I'm afraid of spooking the cardinals. I walk past it each day with my cup of coffee. Sometimes I stand two or three feet away and stare at the female, who pants in the heat as she sits on her eggs. She never flinches at my gaze. The male stays nearby. Except for that one thrasher, none of the hundreds of birds in the yard come near the nest.

Without really thinking about it, I play music more softly now. I switch from percussion and wild yells of lust to the cello suites of Bach.

I would like to introduce you to my family.

We once had a fine home place. The land was rich, the cattle fat, the waters sweet. The women ran through the fair meadows, their dresses flying, their hips flashing joy and lust, their lips tasting of honey. The wine was red, always. We had it all and we fell into our own emptiness.

Hear the swish coming off the women's hips as they run with smiles on their faces? That is the curious part of all this: the sky darkens, the winds roar off the blue water with a new savage force, and joy sits there at the table if we are willing to reach and touch it.

I am standing on a bridge looking into the drowned city, the air rank with the rot of life and a toppled stroller at my feet. The child has vanished and so have all tales of the child. The big wind came through here, the levees breached, and then the healing waters covered all. This was a moment I understood. I have understood for most of my life that the dirt under my feet and the sky over my head will revolt and that a big smackdown is coming, and now I can only note the dawning of this new day. There is no traffic, there are no voices. The only humans I encounter are two cops who say absolutely nothing but stare at me with angry eyes as they guard mile after mile of ruin.

I have come from the lonely towns where no one is left but blank-faced men with guns and lonely dogs snuffling down the empty lanes. The sea grew warm and angry and the city is gone, the people fleeing into the hinterland—I saw their shaken faces in the motels and gas stations for a thousand miles as I careened down the highway coming to this place. I have hardly slept for days and yet I am alert. I have changed, not into a new person but into a final person and this person can only say yes.

Ornithologists have determined that cardinals spend 13 percent of their time eating and about 5 percent flying. This leaves perching, an activity that gobbles up 74 percent of their time. What do cardinals do when they perch?

I sip coffee and the birds feed and then alight on a limb and seem to puzzle out a day mainly singing and scratching their feathers and just staring off into the place we call earth.

In the city of the south, everyone speaks of safety and no one seems to feel safe. The revolution comes nearer in the night. Locals warn that the market should be cleared by nine, ten at the latest. Then the crowds thin, the little stalls are torn down, the danger comes near. So I go. I sit at a table, cold beer in hand, rain glistening on the pavement. A woman spills out of her blouse at a nearby table as her lover strokes her huge breasts. A man drags a cart full of mannequins— the asses exaggerated, the breasts full and with hard nipples. One topples off onto the street and for a few seconds seems alive. Swarms of young males swing through on the prowl. Suddenly cops swarm in, pile out of vans, stand around with automatic weapons. They talk for a few moments and then leave as swiftly as they arrived. It is hard to tell exactly what the police do—setting aside robbing and killing. During the day at this same spot, I saw a man race through the market chasing another man and shouting, "Robber!" Four cops stood nearby in a circle with their backs turned and did nothing.

I turn down a side street and come upon a man patiently working his way through a pile of trash. Two bouncers stand in front of a nearby bar and pay him no heed. I swing onto Avenida Casanova, a street with finer stores and my upscale hotel. Two guys sit on the pavement and tend to their pipes stuffed with *basuco*. One says, "The leader is giving food to people with no future." He sprawls out on cardboard for the night, his head full of *basuco* dreams.

It's two A.M. and the revolution is everywhere, hanging like a cloud, but no one yet has heard the crack of lightning or the roll of thunder. But they wish to believe it is very near in the night.

One educated and very white citizen sizes up the revolution simply: "Before, you got robbed. Now you get robbed and shot. Hate."

White-crowned sparrows come to our yard in winter. Further north, they live at a faster pace; they must eat a seed every four or five seconds in the cold months to survive. Someone has been keeping tabs on them.

Our science watches and projects our own demons. In Maine, the U.S. Fish and Wildlife Service decided to explore the notion of territory. They killed pairs of birds—warblers, vireos. Suddenly there was space available. Pairs of the same species invaded from nearby ground and set themselves up just like their recently dead kinfolk. The study concluded this meant there was a floating population of avian drifters. When homes become abandoned, they move right in.

Thanks to scholars, we have some notion of the cardinal's domain. A Dr. Frank Chapman placed a mirror in the range of a male cardinal. Naturally, the bird went at his reflected image like a samurai. The good doctor kept moving the mirror until combat ceased, at about no feet from the nest.

A cardinal fought and fought another male for his ground, and then he keeled over stone dead. Fortunately, someone was watching, scooped up his corpse and did an autopsy. High blood pressure did him in.

The brown waters slice through the green tangle that lines the river. Here, the billboards of the revolution are impossible to see. Concrete walls trap the river, and ten lanes of road mark the edge of the trees and shrubs struggling in the heart of this city.

The boys call this place La Jungla, the jungle. They watch me with dark brown eyes. The leader is around thirty, and he has shoes but no socks. He leaves at night for a room somewhere, but the boys stay. Their beds of cardboard lean on the slope that runs from the river channel to the road.

Long ago, Columbus entered a big river east of this city. He was stunned by the sweet water and the lush breath of life, the hills teeming with tropical plants and birds, so stunned he thought at first he had found the entrance to Eden, the place where love began and where the first steps of the long fall were taken.

The boys live here but work elsewhere, just across the road in the heart of the city, where office and apartment towers spike against the sky. They root through the city's trash for wire and bottles and clothes to earn maybe a dollar or two a day. They smoke *basuco,* but they deny that they do. The police hunt them at times and sometimes kill them. Feral children are a problem here.

They laugh at some comment. And then their faces collapse again and their mouths become hard lines. Their bodies are smeared with grime and are very lean.

Their leader says he does not like the national leader. I have come to visit the national leader but he is always off touring other nations. The boys' chieftain says the national leader has failed them, has failed in his promises. Maybe he fails because he is surrounded by bad men, but this does not matter, since he has failed to do what he said he would do.

As the chieftain speaks he leans against the guardrail that divides the road from the jungle.

Just across the ten lanes of traffic looms a big hotel with domes on it like out of the *Arabian Nights*. The windows are dark slits. Men with money bring women to this hotel for love. Or they go to the bar and find women for love. The men who pay for these rooms are almost always white but the women can be any color as long as they are willing. They must be willing to smile, to take off their clothing, to lie on their backs, to waggle their legs in the air, to suck cocks, to stand on their hands and knees. And to listen. For this they are paid in either coin or meals or fantasies. They will certainly have large breasts and generous hips. The hair between their legs will be black, the hair on top of their head can be black, blond, or red. They will wear fine scents and no glasses. They will never be over thirty years of age.

Columbus was convinced that the big river to the east flowed from the actual paradise of our ancestors, the one with the tree of knowledge, the one where Eve stood unashamed of her nakedness. I can smell the women in the tower across the road, smell their perfume, smell the juices between their legs. I cannot keep things straight. And this concerns me. But what concerns me more is that I do not try to keep things straight.

I am having trouble with borders.

I keep trying to anchor myself in concrete things. For example, one of the boys is washing his hands and forearms in a five-gallon bucket full of brown water from the river. The sky is blue, horns are honking, from somewhere the boys have gotten five dollies to use to move their bags of trash. Two hundred yards away I can see teenage girls with daypacks crossing a bridge. They will never venture in here, not in their lifetimes. The girls will stay beyond the reach of the boys' eager hands, and the boys will be invisible to them.

That night a light rain floats over the city.

In another market, old men play chess. Three tables away, a woman in her thirties nuzzles a boy of about twenty and strokes between his legs. His hand moves up and down her breasts, the fingers dancing on her brown skin. She is dark and very fat, and her eyes are weary as they kiss. A young guy breaking up his stall glances over at me. He smiles, grabs a mannequin and pretends to fuck it in the ass.

Thirty feet away, young women sit in chairs under a canvas and have their nails done—some red, some white, some a light, ghostly blue.

There is a line and I have crossed it. I believe in the future and I have finally left the past. The problems others mention to me—the poor people, the warming of the gases in the sky, the big winds whipping off the oceans, the beasts dying onetwothreefour like clay pigeons bursting at a skeet range, the wells going dry, the number of people growing and growing, the terror, the energy ebbing and some kind of crisis impending, the bombs, the strange chemicals inhabiting my food and water, the girls, always the girls, the oceans rising, the ice melting, the people migrating and tearing through walls and fences, the cows bearing two-headed calves, the plagues in the warm breeze of each spring—all these things, I ignore. I have entered the future. In the future, things are. In the future, there are neither problems nor those pesky solutions. The river did not lead to earthly paradise, but rather to a cold bottle of beer in the market at night as rain drizzles and women color their nails and smile.

In an abandoned street, cops surge in, mill, and leave. A man sprawls on a sheet of cardboard on the pavement. I sit beside him as he twists foil into a homemade pipe and lights up.

He does not share.

In Arizona, Mexicans used to cage cardinals in order to enjoy the beauty and variety of their songs. The music swells in

February as courtship begins. The birds pair-bond, though strict monogamy seems a ragged effort, with up to a third of the broods in one study resulting from a little fornication on the side. Come spring, the male will feed the female. The nest is built. Life begins again.

This pair seems hardly to leave our small city lot. She sits on a branch. He flies over and lands just above her, singing loudly. When he moves down-limb toward her, she flies away and he follows. The pattern repeats, again and again. Finally he lands above her, slides down, and she does not move. They fuck.

The martini glass glows red in her white hand, the fingers splayed against the funnel shape. Music paws the air, something created with velvet hammers, a sound churning from machines. It is bygone music in a lounge full of young men and women in a fine New York hotel.

The red drink catches my eye. Her lips are red also, as are her nails. Her hair is up, her dress white. It looks like linen but it also looks as if it will never crease. She sits on a man's lap, her eyes glowing into his careless face, which has turned several degrees from her gaze. He appears bored.

Here in the lounge, appetite is sanded smooth.

I sip a ten-dollar glass of red wine. A burly black man in a suit maintains the rope line at the edge of the lounge. The cocktail waitresses are very lean and wear long silken dresses and smile faintly. A large vase holds dry branches. Each room in this hotel opens onto the red-lit atrium. Inside, each has a dial on the wall to make white noise, so that the sounds of the lounge do not interfere with sleep. The walls in the rooms are beige, the furniture simple and lean like the young women selling cocktails. The shampoo and hair conditioner in each bathroom come in small clear bottles shaped like those that once clanked on doorsteps in the early morning hours.

The entire planet seems on hold.

The woman on the lap holds her red drink, her body flush with the man's, hips and legs swiveling into an off angle, a mermaid beached on a sailor's lap. Their upper bodies do not touch. She fingers the glass while his arms hang limp at his sides and never even graze against her flesh.

The red wine flows over my tongue, the sleek waitress bends and asks if I wish for another drink.

The eggs are laid, she sits on them. A predator comes near, a hawk or raven or crow. An alarm is sounded.

Birds of many species may gather to dive-bomb an intruder. And birds are capable of deceit, to defend or to attack. The zone-tailed hawk flies high in the sky, mimicking the carrion-eating vulture, in order to sneak up on prey.

And birds can be opportunistic. Back when such a species existed, a pet passenger pigeon alit on humans whenever it sighted a hawk. Another sought shelter from a peregrine falcon among a cavalcade of mounted men in the Dakotas in 1874.

The dog slips away in the brush. The future is disappearing with the dog's ass, and I scramble, a boy of six or seven, possibly eight. Dead leaves and broken twigs litter the ground, a wet rank odor rises. In my head I am free and have no dream beyond being the dog and being the forest. Everything is in this moment—sky gray, dog moving, the oak leaves and acorns making things slippery underfoot, logs to crawl over, towering white oaks, a small brook knifing through the forest. At the back end of twenty acres, fields begin and the poison of houses lurks nearby.

My father's brother is somewhere behind me in a forty-foot trailer. He's got a glass of Jim Beam, a cast-iron pan on the stove, and he's heating up corned beef hash out of a can, the hash heavy with shakes of black pepper and the steam rising into his grizzled face. I'm following his German shepherd, a vicious dog according to delivery men, strangers, and those who fall out of favor. My uncle is tribal and his tribe holds no truck with casual visitors. Or visitors at all. The dog bites such types. But not me. I am my uncle's namesake and he is a man without child or women, outside of whores. He keeps a .22 Colt Woodsman semiautomatic close at hand. He's done a lot of different work but now it is the cards, the backrooms and money games and a quick hand on the cold metal in his coat pocket.

Twice, to my knowledge, he has beaten men with his hands to the rim of death. There have been charges, but he has slipped past the law. When he was a lineman, he took the full voltage one day but somehow survived. And now he is playing out his hand. By the time I am thirteen he will end it with a bullet from that Colt Woodsman fired into his brain. Kin will make sure I, the namesake, get the gun.

The brown oak leaves, brittle with time, crunch under my feet, acorns make the ground uneasy, and the dog, my God the nose on that beast, the dog tracks a scent in the sweet air. In the evening, my uncle, a miser, tosses dimes into a neighbor's plowed ground and the dog retrieves them without fail. My uncle will die with a hundred thousand cash in a box, die in that trailer with maybe an inch of Jim Beam left in the bottle.

In the valley below, coking mills and oil refineries release fumes into the air, and nearby, prisons huddle. Across the road is the massive limestone farmhouse where I began my life, a place lost to my life when the city took my family into its embrace. The old man planned to be buried in the front yard, but now he is about to peddle the ground out from under my life.

I will never feel comfortable with the word *nature*. Just here, brush whipping my face, a fall now and again, then a scramble after that dog.

Everything must begin somewhere and I think here it begins.

I fall, the dog backtracks, warm breath on my face. Those dark eyes that tell nothing. The nose that misses nothing. I get up and the dog moves forward and I run after it.

Size varies. A golden eagle needs a territory of about thirty-six square miles. A robin manages with less than an acre.

Sometimes, in driving across my city, I would pull in and enter a store where I would find a woman. She would take me into the backroom, safe from the view of customers. Her breasts would spill out of her dress, I would caress them, and we would kiss. In a few minutes I would leave. The first time I met her in her store she helped me with a gift for my girl-friend.

We never discussed my visits or my absences.

It is afternoon, the sun starting to go from white to yellow, when I turn down the lane in a bad neighborhood and find her small house. The front yard teems with a crazy quilt of flowers, as if out of a nineteenth-century print of an English country garden. At the door, she beams. She is a short woman, fine bones, tiny body, and yet at this moment she swells and is full of vitamins and joy and hopes of joy. She is briefly basking in the sunshine of life.

Inside, on a small wooden end table, two glasses and a bottle of chilled white wine wait, beads of moisture forming. She smiles like a pleased child.

She beckons. "Let's have some wine."

I uncork the bottle, pour, and feel the glass cool between my fingers.

The house seems built for an elf and is a statement against the neighborhood of bars, street prostitution, junkies, and trailers where empty beer bottles clink in the trash bins like the ticking of a clock.

We sip.

On each mirror, and there are many, are words: YOU ARE SOMEONE, YOU ARE LOVED, BELIEVE, LOVE, BE LOVED, YES.

The messages are everywhere, all neatly printed in large block letters.

The air is very still and there is no music. Everything is tidy.

We kiss.

She plucks the spaghetti straps on her shoulders and they slide down her arms. Two large breasts peer out.

I say, "No, I can't do this."

I leave.

That night she tries to kill herself.

Years later, I am at a party. A woman of thirty-one tells me that she just ran across something I wrote where I claimed I regretted the times I'd said yes.

Smoke flows off the brisket, I've got red wine in my hand and she is nursing a cold beer.

I offer, "Well, I don't remember writing anything like that. Are you sure?"

She says, "Yes, yes."

And then she disappears.

Twenty minutes later she is back with a book.

She shows me the offending line: I'd written I regretted all the times I said no instead of yes.

She says, "I don't know how I missed that."

The ants come and the bird is willing. It will flare its wings and let them crawl all over its body. It will pick them up one by one, crush them with its beak, and rub them into its feathers. This cleanses and drives out parasites. Or this does something else. No one is certain, but over two hundred species of birds use at least twenty-four species of ants. They also use beetles, mealworms, lemon flesh, orange juice, coffee, vinegar, beer, cigar and cigarette butts (leading to some house fires), hot chocolate, soapsuds, berries, and a couple dozen other substances. One observer saw a bird going through the motions of anting with a snail. A crow has been witnessed standing atop an anthill and letting the insects race over its body. A tame British magpie seized an ant and dipped it in a man's pipe to coat it with ash before rubbing its plumage.

All this I pillage from bird books as I sit and watch the cardinals feed their brood. Two maws reaching up in hunger and parents bring them insects, the pablum of bird life. The drought rolls on.

No one really knows why birds ant. But they do.

I would come out of the desert after hundreds of miles thinking of nothing but fruit pies and women. And then I would go home, shower, and hardly eat for days. Nor bear to speak with anyone, much less caress a woman. The love did this. Night after night watching stars wheel over my body, the fantasy scent of a woman bathing my face, the soft curves of my dreams answered by the rock flooring my bed.

When I read science and natural history, I find no comfort for my lusts. Sometimes I walk out of motels in small towns and cities and move out by foot past the parking lots and big lights, in the darkness go crashing through the brush or mesquite or greasewood and finally settle on some patch of earth. Then I am all right, for a spell.

I cannot abide overhead lights, ever.

I consider campfires a crime.

I make an exception for the sun. I love the sun. It is not an overhead light. It simply is the light.

In Tennessee during a dry spell, a bunch of cardinals—four females and two males—bathed in the heavy dew dripping off sassafras, red maple, and willows. Cardinals also like a good sunbath—wings drooped and open wide, tail fanned out, that crest on the head flared. Sometimes they drink in the rays for fifteen minutes at a crack. All this written off to maintaining feathers, decimating parasites, and the like. We are reluctant to allow birds the motives of a fine woman on a beach.

The yellow light fell through the dirty windows onto the cement floor. I remember the yellow light because where I live it means summer is dying and fall has begun to creep in. I've always hated the yellow light and favored the white glare of deep June. I was somewhere in my late twenties and had, I think, fourteen dollars left.

The woman had left and so had almost all of the furniture and everything else. I was sleeping on that cement floor—I'd ripped up the wall-to-wall carpeting one day because it reminded me of what I never wanted to be. The floor-to-ceiling curtains on the south glass wall had also been torn down and pitched into the alley. The dog had died of the same local plague that had all but finished me off. I'd been unable to work for six months.

So I sat there with my father's .45 Colt semiautomatic, one he'd filched from the army when he was mustered out. He was dead but the gun still had a full magazine. I thought of robbing a convenience store two blocks away.

I had a college education. In fact I'd walked off a job teaching in a midwestern university just a year or two before. Since then I'd driven thousands of miles, trimmed trees and mowed lawns, ghostwritten for a political hack, edited some books, hauled firewood, done two federal research projects, and busted up my marriage. And of course, the dog had died.

For months I'd lain on the floor, feverish and weak with my plague, and slept fifteen to twenty hours a day. I'd been fired for my last federal report just when the wife left and the dog got diagnosed. Then I'd been diagnosed too. I'd run a fever every day for two years.

And then one day, after months on that floor, I got up and walked three blocks, my body sweating like a malaria victim's.

He sends me photographs of giant buses converted into travel homes. The one he has now has a full kitchen, a living area with white leather couches, a bath, and a huge bedroom. I once rode in it for twenty-four hours and was struck by its opulence. But this vehicle is no longer enough, and so he drives a thousand miles to shop for a finer statement.

After the big wind came through and took the city down, I was riding in the night with him and mentioned that there would be more winds, that the seas were rising, the climate changing, the wet places going dry, the ice melting, and not just in my glass. People kept growing in number, the forest was falling down, the fish fleeing, famine and filth and hunger creeping closer and closer.

He said, "I know all that but I don't like to think about it, because what can you do?"

A few months later he started sending me photographs of his new bus.

I learned about the killing days after the drinking. It spilled out of him, a fragment of an experience that he kept carefully tucked away and out of sight, and then suddenly the experience flowed from his mouth and into my mind and there it lodged and would not go away. Sometimes I think about the killing this way: the ribbon unfurls, at first red, then with a black edging growing along the bottom until it devours the red, then a burst of blue, a deep, rich blue drunk with pigment, and finally the blue ebbs into a yellow, sunflower passion as the ribbon dives into the infinity of some dark and starless place.

I was hunched over the cheap tape recorder when the death floated into the air as a hummingbird slurped at the feeder just outside my window on a spring morning. The voice murmurs about a friend, a deep friend, there, this friend, there in a fetal position, and the dead nearby, dead by the hand of the man in a fetal position. The sentence has no subject and the subject in other parts of the tape only appears in the third person, never the first, the whole thing floats without names or dates, drifts out there as if it never happened.

I can see them in my mind, a unit of men that move as one. They know how to proceed, they know their weapons, know each other's smells and quirks and understand the slightest flicker of gestures even in the half-light where the shooting happens.

A body is on the ground. Two men cover the corpse with their own bodies so that ... the dead have privacy. The corpse is one of them, a part of the unit.

None of this is mentioned by the voice murmuring, simply the fact that the friend, the deep friend, kills one of their own.

This is when the ribbon unfurling across blank space turns from blood red to black. I see all this with my eyes open now. I am certain I could reach out and touch this ribbon, it is that real to me.

After the shooting, the man who fired the fatal rounds went into shock and sprawled on the ground in a fetal position.

Black ribbon suddenly gagged my mouth.

You enter the country of the dead. At first you protect yourself by saying the dead are *them* and separate from the vital thing called *us*. Then this boundary erodes and this happens so softly—the sound of a brush kissing a brass cymbal—you seem unaware of the change. Until you sense it, snap alert, look all around, and find you are in the country of the dead, that everyone around you is dead, only some of the dead are still breathing. Perhaps, you have had to take a life. Perhaps, you have seen life taken.

And you cannot speak of this to the innocent, it would ruin their eyes. Not to your colleagues, it is forbidden to speak of it with them because they are strained themselves simply by life in the country of the dead.

That is the way of the country of the dead.

They watch over him in order to stop him from killing himself. He sinks into the dark place. He cannot leave his house. He does not like to talk.

The ribbon begins to slowly shift from black to blue and this shift happens because the pain of the killing retreats. The experts talk about depression and recommend pills.

Eventually they stash him in a place where the work is quieter and the crack of gunfire from the street can never be heard. He is a casualty of the war, and like any decent group of people, his colleagues carry out their dead.

He never makes it to the funeral. He cannot face the family of the man he has killed.

After the killing, when he cannot be left alone, a fellow officer stays at the condo one weekend as part of a shift of people helping out in the bad time. But the cop gets bored and leaves town with one of his women.

Another cop calls and when no one answers the phone, he gets worried. He goes over and finds the man alone, and so morose he will not come to the door or answer the phone or speak at all.

The cop calls two fellow officers, both women, one black of skin and one brown. They come over dressed in miniskirts and thigh-high boots and brilliant yellow tube tops, the decoy costumes of vice officers trolling for johns. One of them picks up a pebble and throws it against the condo window. Then the two of them start boogying on the sidewalk, slapping hands, shaking ass, and flashing perfect white teeth.

Eventually the front door opens, the man emerges, a smile creeps across his face.

That is how he finally begins his journey back.

A big wind has come through the swamps and left fresh life and death in the new waters that flood the land. Around midnight I push the car up toward 100 mph. The police are busy elsewhere or have long fled. There is nothing here to interfere with appetite. The birds have largely disappeared before the big wind. Aerial surveys spot little in the brown, turbid water save alligators, who are suspected to have taken many of the newly dead into their watery world.

He sits beside me with a .40 caliber semiautomatic. His people came to the swamps before my nation had a name.

He turns to me and says into the darkness, "First, they were nigras. Then Negroes. Then they wanted to be called blacks, then black Americans. Now it's African Americans. What do these niggers want?"

I see fallen limbs by the roadside in the glow of the headlights. The area is dark, the power is drowned and nothing works here but wind and water.

Desire.

I am surrounded by it.

He says, "A bartender in the Keys once told me there are two essential traits of successful men: arrogance and a powerful sex drive."

I nod.

He says, "Money motivates people."

The night streams past, the air rich with rot and despair. Houses slip by blind and abandoned, cars are tossed here and there.

We pass an apartment complex. Many of the windows

are gone and curtains trail out into the humid air. A young black woman sits on a chair in front, her face drawn and absolutely blank. Her eyes are dazed, her lips straight as a knife wound. She does not move, seems hardly to breathe. A few days before, at an evacuation center, I saw those same lips on a skinny white woman sitting on a cot, eyes blank, hair lank, hardly breathing.

In a shelter, a black man told me he endured by breaking into white people's abandoned homes. He tells me, "I like eating rich people's food."

He takes me to the secret place in the cold of the mountain morning. I've just met him and his wife the night before at a party in the Black Hills, where the Sioux once lorded it over all creation and where a bullet finally brought Wild Bill relief from his drunken exploration of life. In an overcast sky, slight ribbons of blue bleed light on the clear water. A wild turkey is silhouetted against the canyon wall, neck extended. Early wild strawberries dot the cold soil. His wife, Kate, promises herself to fill baskets come late spring.

Jack has been coming to this slot since he was a boy.

Kate moves easily, constantly stooping to notice first emergence of spring plants, hopping nimbly from stone to stone at the frequent stream crossings.

Jack asks, "Do you mind?" as he hauls out a joint.

The canyon moves in, brushing against my face.

Jack stands by a low dam built of blocks of rock from the canyon floor. When he was a boy, he and friends put it up. The small pond is cold and clear to the bottom. He sits on his haunches and lets the water slip through his fingers. On the stone walls lichen glides—brown, black, yellow, red, green, fingers of color stroking the rock.

I take another hit. The air's too-cold-for-real scent but I imagine the dirt roaring up to my nostrils, the trees exploding and rank with rotting leaves, flies buzzing over still water, at night the moon skating where the canyon slot says sky, and birds in the trees dreaming eggs and hungry mouths, deer ghosting through the brush, no sounds, none, maybe a heartbeat, but still the quiet where a haze of smoke curling off a joint writes thunder words and past and present and future melt and everything comforts the tongue like a good ragù.

Something kindles within me, a breath blowing on an ember, the early tastes of what matters to me glowing, and now a slight flame, that flicker warming within.

When I got arrested in the sixties, I called my father out of courtesy.

He asked, "Is it felony?"

"No."

He said, "Who gives a fuck," and hung up.

She is number 74, just one digit behind me since I am now number 73. Her short blond hair falls lank against her head, her tight hips writhe in low-cut jeans with the blouse riding well above the flat smooth midriff. A stud gleams in her navel. We are visiting the prison, a regular Station of the Cross in life these days.

I'm putting on my shoes as I eye her. I've just emptied my pockets, handed over my footgear, taken off my belt, and made it through the metal detector. I've also signed the standard form in which I promise that I am not carrying metal-cutting tools.

I'm huddled with some Mexican women who have also completed the electronic gauntlet. We sport blank faces, we refuse to chat with the guards or one another.

That is when the blonde sets off the metal detector.

She beams and then stares down at her belly and fondles the stud.

"Yesterday, you didn't say anything," she says to the guard.

Then she fingers the stud, pries it loose and hands it over.

She tries the detector again and still fails.

The guard says, "Must be your bra."

She argues that yesterday the alarm didn't go off.

He ignores her, walks over to a desk, opens a drawer and pulls out a razorblade.

She retreats to the bathroom to cut the wires out of her uplift bra.

I am standing in the yard off the visiting room as my friend talks of how bitter he is and how no one comes to see him except his wife and a few friends and relatives.

The fence framing the patio is about waist high, really just a way to keep visitors and their children corralled. The women I waited with, the ones ready for the visit with their men, are spread along this fence and face it. The men lean back against the fence, their faces blank, and they say not a word.

The women wear overcoats and they splay out these coats with their arms like birds sunning in the early morning light. Their hips move against the men.

The women all smile, the men retain their blank looks.

My friend never even glances over at them.

He tells me no cheap big deposits of oil can logically be left, and that soon the fifty-dollar barrel will be seen as a bargain. The question, he says, is how to play off this reality in the market.

I watch the blonde move her tight ass as she rubs against her man.

The pain ebbs, the stone breaks, I piss gravel. The hotel is now sad, the towers are down, and everyone in this city smells the dead and chants a single date in the calendar. The room has a terrace barred by a locked door. I open a window and crawl out on the cool red tiles. It is night. Across the narrow passageway a man sits in his small living room with a dead antelope head on the wall. He reads. A draped American flag blocks his bathroom window. I've got a bottle and a glass. After the gravel passes, I hobble down to a liquor store on Park Avenue, the one with a color photograph of the towers in the window and the words GOD BLESS AMERICA.

So I drink, have a smoke, let the alcohol calm my body after the spasms. I wait for the smell, the one that comes up at night if the wind shifts and the humidity is high enough. The smell has that undertone of richness that comes from a garden when you turn it over in the spring. But there is a spike of something else, something sharp. People notice on such nights.

The city purrs.

The candles burn in little glass jars at various fire stations, bus stops, random walls of flyers. Such candles should be lit—I have been taught properly—at either seven A.M. or seven P.M., and once lit, they must never be allowed to go out. They are supposed to burn for seven days. But I keep track in my walks, and every candle has blown out. No one is stooping with a match now. Most of the flyers are gone, destroyed by rain or fact.

I take a deep breath, yes, the smell is here.

The flyers mutter.

"... missing finger tip left index finger, 104th floor ..."

The women are dressing well, that is a good sign. The scarf once again goes with the outfit.

"... he wears braces on his teeth for orthodontics ..."

She is coming at me in a tight denim dress, the skirt short, hips tight, bare midriff, yes, still tan. Her hand, the nails red, the fingers long, is half stuffed in the middle of her skirt and tugging it down toward her crotch. Her face is blank, the mask of the streets.

"... he also has a goatee ..."

The first night I crawled out on the terrace through the

window, the hotel had a report of a night prowler. I clarified this error. Now I drink in peace and watch the smoke curl off my cigarette in the lazy air and mingle with that smell.

On my terrace, it is so fine. The velvet night, the red wine, the antelope head staring patiently from the living-room wall across the way, the pain dribbling away from my body. I think of the bruschetta I ate for dinner, how simple and yet how perfect, the flecks of basil exploding with released oil on my tongue.

Even that smell. It is so fine.

I have never gotten the story straight, the tale Jack told me in that canyon in the Black Hills, it's still a jumble of things that make no sense.

It goes like this.

His father gets some bones of a dead Indian from the museum where science placed them long ago. This takes years of letters and demands.

The bones are put in a safe place in the house.

His father suddenly falls ill.

He calls a medicine man he has known since childhood and explains the problem. The medicine man tells him the ceremony. The bones are put to rest in the earth.

He recovers.

I live in a time of fear and the fear is not of war or weather or death or poverty or terror. The fear is of life itself. The fear is of tomorrow, a time when things do not get better but become worse. This is the belief of my time.

I do not share it.

The number of people will rise, the pain of migration will grow, the seas will bark forth storms, the bombs will explode in the markets, and mouths fighting for a place at the table will grow, as will the shouting and shoving. That is a given.

Once the given is accepted, fear is pointless. The fear comes from not accepting it, from turning aside one's head, from dreaming in the fort of one's home that such things cannot be. The fear comes from turning inward and seeking personal salvation.

The bones must be properly buried, amends must be made.

Also, the beasts must be acknowledged.

And the weather faced, the winds and rains lashing the face, still, they must be faced. So too, the dry ground screaming for relief.

There is an industry peddling solutions, and these solutions insist no one must really change, except perhaps a little, and without pain. This is the source of the fear, this refusal to accept the future that is already here.

In the Old Testament, the laws insist we must not drink blood, that the flesh must be properly drained or we will be outcasts from the Lord. They say these rules were necessary for clean living in some earlier time.

I swallow the blood, all the bloods.

I am that outlaw, the one crossing borders.

The earlier time is over.

I watch her pant in the heat as she sits on her clutch. The male comes and goes, bringing her food. The eggs will hatch in eleven to thirteen days. The chicks will begin leaving the nest nine or ten days after hatching. Meanwhile, both adults feed them and clean up their shit.

The fledglings hang around for a month or two and are fed by their parents. Then they are driven off to find their own ground. Sometimes they bunch up with other youngsters and roar about for a spell.

We have a record of a wild cardinal lasting fifteen years and nine months. We also have records that state that only 60 to 65 percent of cardinal adults survive each year.

Something is ending, something is beginning, and this present cannot continue.

I am in the zone of the dead city and the waters are high, the trees windblown and leafless, the faces stark and without pleasure. I kneel in a shelter where they have brought survivors of the big water. Some are white and some are black and their faces are drained of color.

A male nurse tries to explain to himself what he has seen but cannot accept.

A woman with a small child was brought to the shelter. During the big water, during the rescue, during the evacuation, the child's small hand had clung to her mother's arm, clung. The male nurse peeled the child's fingers from her mother's arm, pried them loose one by one. They had made deep gouges in the mother's arm. The mother was unaware of the gouges and unaware of her child's hand. It had become simply part of her body. And as he slowly freed each finger, mother and child stared blankly ahead.

That is what I mean by yes.

I am having drinks in London and an old man who loves jazz tells me of his visit to the city now dead, the city put underwater by the big wind.

He went to a club and a woman sitting at the table next to him leaned over and asked, "Would you like to see my pussy?"

Then she flicked a cigarette lighter and held it over her exposed crotch.

The old man smiles as he tells me this.

I think if God exists he must have a face very much like the old man's as he tells of this moment in the smoky club, when horns blared through the air and the scent of life wafted up.

I will try to explain.

Serpent

A visitor who arrived at the ranch house in May during a bad drought found it coiled in the flower bed by the porch. The rattlesnake, well camouflaged, was all but invisible. My visitor had been squatting to urinate when she noticed it. I was unnerved, but I let the snake be. I was coming off a dark season and had outlawed all guns and all acts of violence from the ranch. It was four or five miles from the Mexican border, and the earth was burning from lack of rain. The snake stayed and eventually moved up on the porch, where it would sleep all day near my chair. It was a western diamondback, the species credited with the most bites and deaths in the United States. I never could tell the snake's sex, but I named it Beulah.

In the dunes, I've put my foot down next to sidewinders. In the abandoned ranch houses of the desert, I've found snakes hanging above the door I'd just entered. I fear them. I have killed them.

Words like *good* and *evil* and *fear* and *doubt* seem nothing to them.

I cannot imagine a snake wondering about the word *yes*.

———

Years later and I am in the Chiricahua Mountains a few feet from a blacktail rattlesnake, one of more than a hundred in a study group. I have entered snaketime.

For the snake a few things are obvious: I am large, and this is certain because of my footfall. She can hear the footfall of a mouse. I am rich in odor. She can pick up the faintest scents, identify them, and follow a single strand as clearly as if it were signage on an interstate highway system. I am clumsy, she can see that with her eyes, though she hardly relies on sight. And I am warm. The pits on her snout allow her to analyze body heat and form an image of it. I become a shape with a field of temperatures of different intensities, one so finely felt that she can perfectly target any part of my body. And I am irrelevant unless I get too close. She will ignore me if I stay six feet away. She will ignore me if I become motionless for 180 seconds.

If I violate the rules of her culture, she will work through a sequence of four tactics. First, she will pretend to be invisible and hope I do not see her. If that fails, she will try to flee. If that fails, she will rattle in hope of frightening me away. And finally, if I am completely ignorant of simple courtesy and get within a foot or so of her, she will attack me. I have failed to observe these boundaries at least a dozen times in my life—I've never been struck but I have caused alarming rattles.

She herself is cultured. In her lifetime, she will attack maybe twenty or thirty or forty times. She will never attack any member of her own species. She will never be cruel. She is incapable of evil.

I never walk my ground without her being in my thoughts. I never make night moves on my desert without an alertness. She never wants to meet me. She never stalks me.

Sometimes I sit in the dark trying to imagine how I look to her. I can only brush against such powers of perception. I cannot hear the footfall of a mouse. My powers of catching scent are feeble in comparison. I can barely sense the presence of others through heat. I am almost always full of aggression barely kept in check.

I have always feared her. That is why I have come here.

I have never wanted to be someone else, I have always wanted to be something else. My life has been spent in the cage of my DNA. There is another country where blood rules, sounds are louder, scent drenches the air, thought flows like a river, flows so calmly that it is not perceived as thought. I imagine the tree at the moment of germination, committing itself to one spot for the rest of its days and nights. Then there is the bird on the wire, the fox darting into the brush, the carp jumping in the creek, a loud slap on the water. What does the jump feel like, what does the sudden burst of light look like, and what is the sensation of a return to beneath the surface of the stream?

I have never believed in a hierarchy of being, with complex organisms up in the tower room and less complex organisms toiling out in the fields.

I have never trusted the word *I*.

I have never felt comfortable with the word *nature*.

That is why I have come to snakes.

I want in.

With Beulah, things began slowly. First I had to deal with my fear. I was in an addled state that spring and I had decided to erase boundaries in an effort to calm myself. Each evening I would put Miles Davis on the stereo, pour a glass of wine, and sit on a chaise longue on the porch in my shorts. Deer would near the house, twirl and make their evening beds. Clouds of bats would come to my hummingbird feeders, and they would hover around my body, brushing my arms and legs and chest and face with their wings. When I arose to refill my glass, the cloud of bats would part, and when I returned they would continue their exploration. Beulah became part of this careless web I was weaving.

If you read this sentence. There, you have done it, and that was longer than a strike, the venom flowing into your tissue, suddenly the sound of the rattle hits your ears and already the fangs have retracted, are once again lying flat against the roof of the mouth, the snake now coiled in repose as you stagger off and wonder if this has really happened to you.

And the Lord says or is reported to have said (Mark 16:17–18): "And these signs shall follow them that believe: In my name shall they cast out devils; they shall speak with new tongues; they shall take up serpents; and if they drink any deadly thing, it shall not hurt them; they shall lay hands on the sick, and they shall recover."

The venom may be clear, the venom may be yellow, or there may be no venom at all. Venom is expensive for the snake to create, and the amount the snake delivers may be metered according to the size of the prey or whether the snake is seeking to kill something to eat or simply trying to protect itself from danger. We don't really know. We have hospital statistics on dry bites, but we have no idea how accurate they are. Some people when bitten will wait to see if they can handle the reaction because of the expense of visiting a hospital.

We know that rattlesnake venom is a witches' brew that attacks both tissue and nerves. Swelling results, paralysis results and eventually the organism ceases to breathe. The venom also delays the rot of tissue, probably an aid in digestion since rattlesnakes eat so infrequently they need a few hours to fire up their guts to handle chow. The venom also taints the target with a special scent that enables the snake to track the rat or rabbit that bounds away and to distinguish its scent from all those other rats and rabbits in the area.

What is clear is this: A human bitten by a rattlesnake will

usually survive. And a human bitten by a rattlesnake will never wish to repeat the experience.

I have a photo on my wall of a rattlesnake clutching an acorn woodpecker on the back of the neck. The bird is held with its body perpendicular to the snake's mouth. The gleam in the woodpecker's eye makes it clear it is still alive. Venomous snakes generally hold on to birds, since if they fly away they will leave no scent trail on the ground for the snake to follow. The snake's eyes are also open and its seven fine rattles are visible. The snake swallowed the bird over two and a half hours, without ever changing the position of the bird in its mouth. At some point during this meal, the venom killed the bird.

The photograph captures much of our horror of snakes: The slaughter of the innocent, the terror we have of being swallowed alive. The slit of the unblinking snake's eye, the sense of impending death that somehow radiates from the woodpecker. The sense of otherness that snakes evoke in us each and every time.

I have noticed over the years that love of nature often leaves skid marks on the ground when it comes to snakes.

There is no way to be absolutely safe. In the spring, a four-year-old girl wandered with her mother near my town into a canyon that is a favorite nature preserve. The child reached down near a rock and was instantly struck by a rattlesnake. She survived after setting a new record for the antivenin infusion, forty-four vials.

The girl later said, "Maybe the snake had babies and she was trying to protect them."

Not probable at such a season. The girl had, most likely, accidentally transgressed the four stages of the snake's culture and arrived instantly at the last station, attack.

The girl is not the typical victim. In Arizona, the classic snakebite victim is a male who was drinking and decided to show off by pestering a snake. During one recent decade in the state, there were 1,912 bites from rattlesnakes and four deaths. In the foothills near Tucson where the four-year-old was bitten, the rural fire departments remove several thousand rattlesnakes a year from the lots of complaining homeowners.

For thousands of years, human contact with rattlesnakes in the wild has gone like this: we collide with rattlesnakes or we have no contact with them at all. It is as if we based our entire knowledge of automobiles on head-on collisions.

Rattlesnakes hardly make a mark on human numbers. But there is always this edge: you can never be absolutely safe. And this zone of fear has become what rattlesnakes are to almost all human beings.

I have always wanted out and seldom been able to pin down precisely what I sought to escape. Drugs have proven insufficient for my getaway. I have failed twice at marriage and repeatedly at other arrangements. I have seldom held down a normal job. Drink has always been a temptation kept at bay only by a murderous work ethic. There has also been a yen for violence.

Here, I'll show you. I am moving down that road. Patience is wearing thin. Night has dropped like a ton of bricks but still the truck roars on. The new bottle was hard to crack what with the driving, but now it's open. I take down the red wine in gulps. Out there hums a marvel of modern times, the Black Mesa electric trolley, a train that carries coal from Black Mesa to Page, Arizona, the town cheek to jowl with Glen Canyon Dam. Behind the dam, under the waters of Lake Powell, sleep no dead canyons. The train hauls endless cars of coal to the power plant at Page, which helps generate the juice to make everything run in these and more distant parts. Decades have passed since the last nail was driven in the coffin, and the train works day and night moving those tens of thousands of tons of fuel to keep the beast fed. I take another swig and tell myself I can't run the world. Big wires keep on humming. The window is open and the desert breeze feels warm and rich with night scent. It is good to be alive.

The truck moves very fast on the snakelike road crossing the Navajo ground. The coal train purrs along on the tracks parallel to the road. The flash from the barrel is alarming, the brilliant yellow flame and then the smell of gunpowder. The bullets strike the cars full of coal with a dull thud. Any fool could hit them. I contemplate metal-jacketed rounds from a larger caliber, which would penetrate the walls of the cars and might ignite the coal.

The entire exercise is pointless. But I breathe more easily now.

The stretch of road is one where Navajos die in drunken incidents. It is rumored to be haunted by their ghosts, the terrifying Navajo wolves. One is warned not to pick up hitchhikers on this stretch, particularly at night.

I have been walking out the door on peace and quiet most of my life. I keep thinking that I will get older and calm will descend. A white picket fence surrounding a perfect cottage will appear. I will pull over, park, walk into the yard, open the door, enter, and feel the balm.

I feel calmer living with a rattlesnake underfoot. No one warned me this might happen.

As the weeks went by, I began to notice little facts about Beulah. I would be out on the porch in the blazing heat, with no cooling at all, and she would be curled by my chair as I read. I'd get up and go get another glass of water, and she would not stir. She was coiled but seemingly at peace.

I rummaged through my limited snake lore, the various

myths that different cultures had employed to deal with serpents. I noticed a common feature, whether they saw snakes as good or evil: snakes possessed potential menace. The Christian version, with its Garden of Eden, serpent, and apple, baffled me the most. I could never understand how knowledge was part of any fall from grace. With Beulah, I learned to move slowly, out of courtesy.

The front door is open. On the floor sits my armory of shotguns, rifles, and pistols. My Great Pyrenees stands over the guns. I have been on the road for a week or so. (I left him a slit fifty-pound sack of dog food and ample water from a toilet in the shed. He has free run of my property.) There is no telling when the break-in occurred. The dog glares at me briefly, then turns and goes out into the yard. His shift has ended.

I am enraged. I grab a .45 semiautomatic pistol from the pile and race outside. I find no one. I charge into the alley. I have no doubt I would have shot and killed anyone I found on my city lot.

I cannot imagine anger in a rattlesnake. Defense yes, aggression yes. But not this deep anger that rolls through me at times without rhyme or reason. From what we know, a snake has a home range but not a territory. It lives and knows intimately a patch of ground but makes no effort to defend this patch from interlopers. Nor has a rattlesnake any functional definition of *interloper*.

This is the open door I seek from my prison, the one that leads to an otherness. There is a raft of words—nature, the environment, biology, ecology, herpetology, ornithology, conservation, wilderness—I use to mask my interest because such terms are acceptable and my appetite is not. We are taught to study other forms of life and I often read books in pursuit of this goal. I resist science even as I swallow science whole.

The door is open. I have been sitting on the couch reading

a book. There is a knock and so I rise. She enters with a sideways glance. She is not expected. No one is expected. It is a Sunday afternoon, the light still bright outside in the yard. I am wearing a T-shirt and running shorts and clutching that book. I get coffee, we sit on the couch. In the past, we have done business together and had drinks. I do not know where she lives, I am ignorant of her life. She always has a scent like soap, talks quickly with a clip to her words. She is short and trim. Her eyes are quick and wary, she seldom smiles or laughs. Life is a series of oppressions, I sense rather than know this.

She stands in order to take her empty cup to the kitchen. I put a hand on each hip and turn her toward me. I press my face against her crotch and inhale. I slide her shorts and panties off and bury my face in her hair. She moves to set down the coffee cup.

We do not speak.

The ragged lip of her vagina, the salt, hair against my lips. I take off my shirt, she sucks my cock. The light is cool and seeps through the louvers of the shutters, the skin on her back smooth, her long hair flowing off one shoulder. She is on her back, tongue in mouth. Music softly plays from the living room.

Her ass against my hips, the scent at the nape of her neck, fingers brushing against her nipples.

There are clinical measurements of pulse, hormones, blood flows, fluids.

We cease moving, breathing slows, the skin wet.

We part. The feeling fades and becomes words.

We are a filter guarding ourselves from ourselves.

The door closes.

Love is the engine, the only thing that matters, the sensation that moves the planet down some path that makes today look less than tomorrow. And love is not remembered. The wars, the rich, the bluesmen beating their women, the long drag off that joint, the killing ground, these get remembered. Along with famines, plague, and those other two horsemen riding death through the duly recorded pages. But not love. It simply moves things. All the forgotten mothers. And lovers. And eager lips facing down history and reaching for warmth amid the cold stars of midnight.

I believe this. But I cannot clearly tell you what love is.

It can look like this in field notes: *"21 F [female] 0700, Moved 10 M [meters] E [east] in 1 d [day]."* Down by the creek, the ash and sycamore and mesquite and oak melt into a cool green, the ground breathes from summer rains, and the snakes are underfoot with the time of August mating. The rats are plentiful and killing comes more often now. The humidity makes my shirt limp, and clouds bunch around the peaks each afternoon.

I believe absolutely in the notes, in the manner of the notes, in the need for the notes and in the science that will spring from the notes someday like young corn. But what I feel is the creek bottom in August, the possibility of a snake coiled underfoot. I smell things more than I think as I walk the bottom with the dappled light making the ground a mosaic where anything can hide in plain view.

I want to walk across a bridge to a place where the loneliness ends, a bridge framed by trees and with a meadow beckoning on the other side and then beyond the meadow and the songs of larks is a hill and I climb the hill and go down the other side into the desert where we know ultimate matters are revealed and the snakes are everywhere.

I want to know what that feels like. I want to go there, across that bridge, past that meadow, up that hill, and down into that distant country so very near at hand.

———

The rain lifts on the rim country and the ground steams in the fresh sun. He's standing out in front of the tribal gambling hall at seven A.M. smoking.

"Where you heading?" he asks.

"Whiteriver."

"Can I get a ride?"

"Sure."

He's not too drunk and for a big man he moves with grace. I fire up the machine as he pulls a malt liquor from his pocket. He rolls down the window and lets the forty-degree chill of morning splash his face. He's been down seven and a half in federal prison—something about assault on the cops and a matter of drug dealing. But he got out a little over two years ago and he's clean now, clean like spring water.

I ask him how the killings are around here. He tells me twelve murders in the last two weeks. Maybe one in four get reported, he allows.

Spruce and fir float past the window. The woods here teem with bears and elk. It's high ground, with the sacred peak topping out at eleven thousand and hundreds of miles of trout streams and a few dozen lakes.

"I can show you beauty places," he says as the road spills off the rim and floats down a canyon to the river.

When he speaks, his tongue flows almost like a viper's through the gap of missing teeth on both jaws. His eyes are glazed but quick.

He gives me a brief tour of the villages and their preferences for cocaine or meth or heroin. He deals with Anglo suppliers only. He's not fond of Mexicans, but then his people waged war with them for about 250 years. In those days a guy like him could run nine-minute miles for hours through this broken country.

In his language, the word *ni'* has two meanings: Mind. And land.

He kills off one can in about five miles and whips out another from the pocket of his big black overcoat.

"Do people here bother the bears?"

"Naw, not unless they come round a house. Then, they pop them."

The people are often around the house since there are no jobs.

"Bear meat is sweet," he adds.

We pass a woman with fine hips, long black hair trailing down her back to her ass.

"Umm, I like that. Course, I don't force anyone," he confides.

A week or so before, at a party, three guys took a woman in her twenties into the bathroom and stomped her with their steel-toed boots. Then one of them whipped off his leather belt and strangled her. They buried her out back and returned to partying. She left three kids.

He warns me about a town off the reservation. "The Mexicans are rampant there, rampant."

His people have been here for at least five hundred years, maybe more, nobody is really sure. They've hung on to their core ground, more than a million and a half acres, with thirteen thousand official tribal members. The ground runs off mountains and flows with rivers, turkeys outnumber the tribe, bears and elk are everywhere, and the streams boil with trout. His people once believed the trees and shrubs were hair, the rock and mountains bone, the streams blood, and the wind the earth breathing. Some of the old people still do.

He tells me his name and says, "Don't tell anyone that name around here, you'll get in trouble."

And then after a spell he says, "Tell them my name and they will be afraid."

They are right over there in the shelter of the rock on this hillside on the eastern flank of the Chiricahua Mountains near the Arizona and New Mexico line. I am sitting on the ground six feet away. The two pregnant females are piled on top of each other, the section of their bodies where the fertile eggs are lodged exposed to the sun. The rest of their bodies cool in the shade. The sunlight and the heat of their bodies on each other will hasten gestation and accelerate birth.

I'm with my herpetologist friend Dave Hardy, who is busy making notes. He carries gear on his back for tracking the study population, each of which has been surgically implanted with a transmitter and antenna. This means two simple things: the subjects can always be found by their individual signals and the subjects are almost never alarmed. In the fifteen years of the study, there have been few displays of aggression except when the subjects have been grabbed for battery changes, a maintenance task that must be done every eighteen months. So far Dave and his partner Harry Greene have amassed thousands of field observations of *Crotalus molossus,* blacktail rattlesnakes.

What Dave and Harry have found is a separate nation unlike our nation. We see rattlesnakes as menacing, simple-minded eating machines. In more than a decade, the study has witnessed only one kill. An adult female, No. 21, was coiled and in hunting alert when a cottontail came by. She struck it in the left shoulder. The rabbit jumped into the air and ran about twelve feet away, paused, and started making distress cries and spinning in circles. No. 21 returned to her hunting coil. The rabbit ran about twenty feet farther and the rattlesnake slowly began pursuit, following the scent trail. For the next two hours Hardy followed the snake as she followed the rabbit. Sometimes the snake would get within three feet of the rabbit before it would tear off again. When Hardy came back the next day, the snake had a bulge, undoubtedly from swallowing the cottontail. She stayed in place for eleven days, and then on September 1 moved about thirty feet to the east. The flash of the strike, and then the endless ribbon of languor that seems to be snaketime. After about a half-hour Dave and I stand and move off. He flips his radio receiver to another frequency and we go to visit with another rattlesnake. The two females are still, as if we had never existed or mattered to their world. When I look back I cannot even make them out on their rock ledge.

It cannot simply be the venom, or the rattle, the sensation of brushing one's fingers against the scaly hide. Everyone knows they will come for you in the night, seeking warmth, as you sleep out under the stars. You will awaken to the rattle and the fangs raging into your flesh. Nineteenth-century travel guides for pioneers recommended surrounding one's bedroll with a hair rope, an insuperable barrier to serpents.

I have slept hundreds of nights on the desert floor without a tent, and I have never been bitten. Nor have I ever met a person who found a rattlesnake in his bedding. But still this dread—of a furtive reptile that warns us if we get near and flees our presence as if we were death incarnate—persists.

From what deep emptiness does this dread arise?

During the Second World War, the zookeepers of London made provisions for the lions, the rhinos, their various wards. Except for the venomous snakes. Those they slaughtered lest they escape during a bombing attack.

The eye does not blink, the tongue flickers, the body is long and undulates across our skin. We dread.

I have no future. A war threatens to suck me in, my schooling has become a curse and so I flee. For work, I find a factory, and six days a week I drive an hour each way and then walk into its dull light and smooth efficiency. The building is full of computers to aid us in building yet more computers. The moments all feel like ropes tightening around my body. I, who dreamed of being a farmer, now spend most of my hours in a factory and see trees as things slipping past my window on the freeway.

To cope, I drive too fast, I travel for hours on my day off, I try to read. I cannot write. I wait for the war and work in the factory.

On my third day at work I score a lid of marijuana. I enter the clean room where the huge computers live in pure air and constant temperature and I light a joint. Sensation clatters through my mind, the crash of surf, scent off a forest floor, the taste of coffee in the fog of dawn in a small valley nestled in coastal mountains, the feel of fresh crab in my mouth, clean and sweet.

I will never forget the dread. Not of the war, nor of the factory. But of living my life and yet having my life pass me by.

After that, it was clumsy, it was indirect, but it was always a search for the place where I could go to the snakes.

I began to worry about Beulah's diet. I looked closely at her each morning, hoping to see a bulge from some kill made in the night. I wondered at times whether it was the house that drew her, a disruption in the soil that makes good habitat for rats. Or maybe it was the drought, even though I knew that rattlesnakes have low moisture needs and hardly need to eat for that matter. But mainly, I did not think about it at all.

A great horned owl along the wash roosted each day by a trail I took. At first the owl would break cover when I went by. Slowly its reaction time narrowed and it would take off only at the last moment. Finally it ignored my daily passage completely. I became like the owl and slowly adapted to Beulah.

I have taken tobacco, alcohol, meth, LSD, cocaine, hashish, marijuana, coffee, tea, maté, Percodan, and bootleg concoctions. My knowledge is limited but sincere. Day has become night, cotton has turned to velvet, scent has become a hurricane of sensation bathing my face. There have been long speed-fueled drives that go on for days and two thousand miles. None of them have gotten me out of my own hide. The visions turn out to be vapors.

I have sat late at night in Mexico with my hand on a rock seeking messages. They do not come, or if they are being sent, I cannot comprehend or decode them. I have crawled on my belly following various beasts of the field for hours, trying to enter the rhythm of their lives. I have made friends with songbirds, hawks, owls. Fish have scurried across ponds to my hand in hopes of food.

I have also tried to live with the insects—bees, spiders, scorpions, ants, and the like.

Time has been spent with trees.

These encounters have simply reinforced my sense of solitude. I am baffled by the literature proclaiming some deep communion with nature. In my travels toward other bloods I have simply learned how feeble my perceptions are.

It was the spring of my freshman year in high school. The sun fell brightly on the Arizona desert where I was camped with a friend. Deer came and went across the corners of our eyes. A herd of javelina exploded before us as we wandered through a thicket of mesquite. The sap was rising in the trees and in my life. I carried a .22 Colt Woodsman in a holster I'd cut and fashioned from the hide of a steer. I carved flowers of my own design into the leather and stained it a rich red-brown. The gun had come into my life after my uncle used it to commit suicide.

My earliest memory on earth is this: I am two—because of quirks of my life I can date the memory exactly—and my mother is hanging clothes on the farm in Illinois. The sky aches a deep blue and the grass stands taller than I do and floods the air with a rank green scent. I see something slithering, toddle after it into the grass. My mother screams and grabs me. That was my first snake and the first moment I remember of life. Later, say from two to three, I fabricated that imaginary companion so common in children. In my case, a snake I rode like a horse about the countryside.

I grew into a boy who feared snakes, felt uncomfortable in their gaze, recoiled from the few times I'd touched them. That is the fourteen-year-old stumbling down the Arizona wash with his friend and his pistol in the hopes of springtime. We come to a deep cut in the arroyo where the clay bank forms a cliff maybe twenty feet high above the sand bottom of the dry bed. I climb it as a lark, hand over hand.

About fifteen feet up, I take hold of a shelf and pull myself higher with both hands. As my head rises above the shelf, a dozen diamondbacks rise up from coils, tongues flicking, heads and necks seeming to weave back and forth. I instantly stand off into space and fall to the wash below. I can taste the fear in my mouth, and then anger. I get to my feet and scout out the small dirt cliff. I work around to the west so that I come across the rattlers from above. I empty the clip, reload from my cartridge belt, and empty it again. I kill them all.

We skin them out and keep every decent-sized rattle. Later, we show the trophies to girls at school.

I was well past voting age when I understood what I had stumbled upon. Diamondbacks, unlike blacktails, will den together over a winter. Come the warm breath of a spring day, they will emerge into the sun to warm their bodies.

Their faces still sway before me, the tongues flicking for scent, the rattles going, the eyes trying to piece me together, the heat-sensing pits by their noses delineating this ball of heat that suddenly looms before them.

The arts also fail me. Words I know too well to trust. The skeleton of grammar creates a wall that wards off sensation. Sex can only be described sequentially, one stroke after another. Vocabulary discerns distinctions, just as hormones sand down such matters. The visual arts frame things so that they are safe. Dance is the twitching of the body of one species. Music, I still retain hope for music, that bath of sound that words can barely describe and seldom add to. Music echoes with the bark, the grunt, the trilling, the scream, the explosion of the volcano, the purring of the stream.

Art seems less an open door than a gilded cage. Van Gogh painted about three hundred canvases during his year in that nut house. The others, the splattering expressionists and impressionists and cubists and dada folk and surrealists, they're safe. A dripping clock can never punch you in the face like crows rising off a wheat field. I think most of human art and all of human costume results from our notorious discomfort with our own skins.

The patterns of snakeskin are the envy of textile designers. The rattle moves at forty to seventy cycles a second and generally has a pitch between a C and C-sharp. The snakes' state of grace is not a performance but a life. We struggle for style, they are born a style. We struggle for mannerism, they live a court etiquette where every expression of being is as severely restricted as the sequence of a Japanese tea ceremony. I do not think snakes make art. I think they live art. There may be little innovation but there are no faltering or loutish moves.

Snakes are alert to what is out there. The smell of this world, the play of light, the sound of a faint footfall, the sky, and the sun. And certainly the moon, given the hours they keep. But it is impossible to think of neurosis in a snake. They live in a great amphitheater of sensations, we live in a stale closet of concerns. Of course, we are also wily. We make a great fuss of this thing we call Art and insist that it distinguishes us from other organisms. We relentlessly track its origins in figurines of fat women, scratches on bones, paintings in caves, and the arrangements made for our dead. If Art matters, it matters simply as an indicator of how seldom we see or feel or touch or taste or flick our tongues against the endless parade coursing through the air.

I sometimes think Beethoven willed himself into deafness so that he could finally taste the vibrations playing across his flesh.

One day, someone I had not seen in years came to the ranch, an old friend from high school. He'd gotten deep into Eastern religions and had just come back from a pilgrimage to India and Nepal. By that season the great horned owl had mated, built a huge nest just below the ranch house in a cottonwood along the wash, and now the two of them had a clutch of hatchlings to feed. For a week or two I'd been sprawling on the ground with a drink in the late afternoon as I watched the owls. I sent my friend down to see the birds and the nest while I stayed up at the house on the hill and cooked dinner. The owl instantly attacked him and knocked the hat off his head.

I realized he was a stranger to the owl.

That is how I began to relate to Beulah. She was not a pet but somehow I was part of an accepted landscape. She coiled next to my chair as I read in the heat of the afternoon. I moved slowly so as not to alarm her. We seemed to learn each other's ways.

Dogs first beckoned me into the kingdom of other bloods. My earliest memories drip with the tongues of dogs lapping my face. The smell of their fur is likely to be my last memory on earth, as will be the mystery of a dog's eyes—open, friendly and yet a barrier to what the dog thinks. They move in the darkness, go into the forest, howl at the moon, live in a place we know only by their visits to our fires.

I have cradled too many dogs as they died and seen them look at me without fear but with a kind of condescension as they slid into a void we fear to even contemplate. Dogs were my first clue about my limits. And my first guides to the rim of this other place.

I have always been struck by the contempt held for dogs as we adamantly insist they are protohumans joining our families. We give them names, assign them natures, note with delight their quirks, mock their befuddlement when they face the machines that now fill our lives. And turn a blind eye to their pissing and shitting, their nuzzles in our crotches, their fascination with stench, their willingness to hunt down other forms of life.

The first dog was named Dick. Right now I can smell his fur, the tongue licking my two-year-old face. I never knew what he was thinking. That much the dogs have given me.

The woman in the gray suit leans against the white wall as rays of Wisconsin light fall strangled by gray scud and crawl across the polished oak floor. She tells me I am mentally ill and need therapy, and she should know, she's the state-paid house shrink. Her hips are wide and she wears flats. My white MGA, a two-seat ragtop with one window gone, is parked outside with all of my possessions, a suitcase, some books, and a typewriter. I say nothing.

If I walk out on the university I will almost instantly lose my scholarship, my future in the professoriate, and my draft-exempt status.

If I stay, I will wind up giving advice just like the woman in the gray suit leaning against the white wall.

I drive.

Increasingly, when people came out to the ranch, I noticed that Beulah disappeared. If no one came, she'd stay out there with me in the inferno of the afternoon. But when I heard a car pull up, the clunk of the doors, and then arose to see who had come, Beulah would be gone from her post by my chair when I returned.

I began to wonder if she could tell me apart from other people.

For a long time the desert was nothing but snakes to me. When I slept on the ground in the desert, I thought they would come for me. When I walked the summer nights, I imagined them out there, coiled and ready to strike my flesh and fill me with poison. Once, I crossed a dune and repeatedly put my foot down near coiled sidewinders half buried in the sand. Ribbons of snake tracks covered the swells. At dusk, I threw my bag down and slept, the sleep of surrender. I think that marked the turning point, the moment when I grasped two facts: that there was nothing I could do about the snakes and that none of the snakes in my desert were hunting me, because I was too big to swallow.

One June midnight when the air runs ninety degrees, I stumble through the desert without a trail. My pack weighs a good seventy to eighty pounds. My bare legs bleed from small scratches left by thorns, and no matter how much I drink I am sinking into dehydration. This is when I step on the rattlesnake. The sound of the rattle, the feel of the snake under my running shoe, my movement away—all this is a single memory. The snake does not strike and remains coiled. I sit down a few feet away and stare at it in the half-light of a world revealed by stars.

I ceased to think of snakes as enemies. I started thinking of them as part of something I dimly belonged to. They were not my friends, they were not my enemies. They were not like me: they simply were.

I lost interest in their mouths with the two long fangs that could inject venom into my tissue. I began to consider them another nation, one with a culture about which I had not a clue.

There are lines we are warned not to cross. Ethics teaches us we cannot consider other life forms as things. Science teaches us we cannot project our human nature onto other living things. I am from another place. I am not like the snake. But I am not below or above the snake. I lack any sense of hierarchy in the natural world, regardless of the charts drilled into my head since boyhood of the odyssey of evolution. I don't see my species as the culmination of anything, nor do I look at a rattlesnake as a failed ancestor.

That night in the long-ago June heat, the air is dry in my nostrils, the snake stays coiled, I drink water, and the safe ground formed by the beliefs of my people erodes out from under me. I continue for years to move at night across the desert floor. A part of me is never relaxed, another part of me is always resigned.

I do not accept rattlesnakes. That attitude would have me assuming a power that is beyond my reach or my right. Rattlesnakes do not need my approval. Sometimes people ask me about problem snakes hanging around their houses and threatening their dogs and themselves. I tell them if they move the snakes less than two miles, they will be back. If they move them more than two miles, the snakes will slowly starve to death, robbed of their home-range knowledge. I tell them to live with them or kill them.

Some years back a woman was horseback riding near Phoenix when she fell on a rattlesnake, took a hit with massive venom into an artery and died. That is just as likely to happen to me as to someone who hates every snake on earth.

As dusk deepened at the ranch that spring and early summer, the roar of hummingbirds at my feeders on the porch never slackened. I had about ten species and a population of hundreds, exactly sixty-four at a time feeding at any given moment, and a waiting mob swirling around them. Orioles would come also, and I delighted in the clack of their bills as they devoured honeybees on the feeders.

Beulah was seemingly oblivious to this roar of life. She

appeared to sleep through the day—though to my knowledge no one knows by any brain-wave study if rattlesnakes really sleep. But as night came on, at that moment when the sun was down but I could still see, she would uncoil and slowly slither across the porch, passing within inches of my foot, tongue flicking and body undulating. Once, she actually crossed my bare foot. She would go down the steps and vanish into the wild grasses and then be gone from my view. When I arose in the morning, I would find her at first light by my chair. I never knew where or why she went—I assumed her expeditions were about hunting. But that was a part of her world locked off from me.

I have repeatedly engaged in foolhardy and dangerous activities in an effort to punch past the borders. I have run rapids, scaled cliffs, staggered up mountains, crossed glaciers with their beckoning crevasses, tested riptides, swum with feeding sharks, spun off blue highways like a helicopter rotor flying into the blackness of night. Carried guns, been in bad rooms where everyone had a machine pistol and a business concern. Felt the heavens as a small aircraft sought a break in the cloud cover and then put down on some bumpy patch of dirt amidst the jagged rocks of the sierras. The long desert crossings also come to mind.

My behavior baffled me because I knew that I was a coward and feared violence and physical pain as much as, if not more than, others fear such things. I have no appetite for fistfights, less for killing. I do not like being lashed by storms fifty miles from shelter. The sea and its depths make me cold with fear. I have been underwater as sharks raced past, mouths agape, feeding off schools of fish.

I am convinced all of my moments of risk were self-created in order to escape the deathly feeling everyday life gives me. I cannot seem to feel alive unless I am alert and I cannot feel alert unless I push past the point where I have control.

Once, a whirlpool pulled me to the bottom of a river. Looking up at the bright surface as it receded and the darker waters closed around me, I thought I had finally done it and now I was going to die.

The whirlpool coughed me up, I floated away on the surface, my lungs gasping for air.

I always think other things can hurt me. I seldom think other things will hurt me. And so I go. I crawl on the ground with a blacktail rattlesnake as it moves silently along the creek bottom, flicking its tongue against the same air I inhale.

The year neither begins nor ends. There is no harvest moon, no appointment calendar. Time is a ribbon, or perhaps time is a moment. There is a future tense, the snake coils by a game trail and waits for prey. So there is a future. The past is beyond our speculation. We simply cannot decide if a rattlesnake has a past. Except that there are clues: young eastern timber rattlers have been observed following the trails of adults and moving into their various hunting stations a day or two behind them. Is this learning? And if something is learned, does it constitute a past?

Blacktail rattlesnakes have home ranges roughly two hundred meters wide and five hundred meters long in the study area. Their inability to survive when displaced from their home range implies that they know the resources of their home range, which in turn implies that they learned those resources, which in turn implies that they have a remembered past. Snakes that are moved from one place to another tend to keep cutting right angles, as if they were looking for some known geography, perhaps a horizon line. In the years of the blacktail study, only two or three blacktails have entered the study area from outside the mapped home ranges. Does this mean the group in the little valley is some genetic pocket, a tribe perhaps? We don't know.

Blacktails live in a world with little temperature variation. The winter dens run in the sixties; outside, they use sunlight or shade or holes in the ground to keep their blood at a fairly constant heat. Being cold-blooded means that they cannot generate their own heat, not that they are cold. In the study group, each individual eats one to two wood rats a year. In hard times, they can skip eating for a year or more. Given a life span of twenty-plus years and the speed of a strike, this suggests that the strike—that image burned into human consciousness—is a minor part of a blacktail's life, adding up to a minute at most. The barnyards would rejoice if human appetites were so restrained.

Hardy and Greene are closing in on four thousand field observations of their colleagues and in all that time have seen two strikes—one successful, one a miss. Mainly they find the snakes moving slowly or inert. Blacktails have no conflict with each other or with other rattlesnakes. Once they reach some size at age two or three, almost nothing tries to kill them. They live a life with acute sensitivity to the world around them, slight food needs, almost no climatic stress, and huge swatches of time.

That is the brute life of a blacktail: sensation, time, lack of stress, scent, color, and light.

The partly overcast sky dapples the hillside above the creek. From the radio receiver beeping in Dave Hardy's hand, I know No. 39, a female, is very near, but still I cannot see her. She is in the middle of a wash, clearly outlined by the gravel and sand and near a dark limestone rock when I finally make her out. She is coiled, rattles tucked out of view, head held slightly back, the classic hunting posture. No doubt she is by some game trail detected by her fine sense of smell. We know male snakes can figure out which way a female snake has gone by noticing the scent differences on each side of a blade of grass or a pebble where she passed. A bug lands on No. 39, she flinches ever so slightly, then goes still again in her camouflaged ambush posture. Rattlesnakes must wait for prey, they cannot run it down. Which raises an interesting question: How much time do they spend hunting?

They are normally coiled in order to save body heat and so to our eyes almost always appear in a hunting posture. They are often poised by a game trail, but then they must be somewhere, so why not by one of the many strands marking the earth that rats have created? They appear sleepy and yet alert. Harry Greene kept a bushmaster, a huge Central American viper, in his lab. The snake was like a pet rock in its cage; it never seemed to move. And yet when Harry tossed in a mouse every month or so, the bushmaster invariably caught it in midair. Imagine that state of rest and yet alertness. So far, we lack the words for such a state, and certainly we lack any analogy in our own experience. What does hunting mean to an animal that hardly eats?

No. 39, like all the snakes in the study, has a known and mapped home range, a winter den (blacktails winter either alone or with one or two others), a birthing den, and a known pattern of travel from each site to the creek where in August the rats are thick and the mating season occurs in what seems a little like a blacktail Woodstock. In the courtship season, males hungrily follow the scent trails of females, sometimes traveling five hundred meters a day. Their testosterone levels also rise during the mating season. The scientists managed to capture and equip with transmitters all but two of the snakes in the study by finding lusty males in the company of already outfitted females during the mating season, or following outfitted males to females. The famous combat of rattlesnakes, where two males rise, intertwine, and fight for females, is more like arm wrestling. The larger male invariably knocks down the smaller male and wins, with no physical damage involved. Copulation can go on for a day or more—Dave and Harry have been known to tire and pack it in sometime after the twentieth hour. The sperm is stored, the eggs fertilized the following spring, the young born live, three or four in a litter. The mother stays with the young until they shed their skins and can see—this takes about two weeks. Apparently, almost none of the young survive, and the females generally go two or three years between birthings. But then blacktails, with their long life spans, require a very low replacement rate.

In the fall, the snakes migrate uphill in the valley to their winter dens and largely stay within them until spring. That is the year for a blacktail.

We go down the hill to the creek and find No. 34, a female, basking in the sun. Three days ago she ate, and the bulge is still clearly visible. No. 46, a male, glides up and down the rocks of the creek bank about fifteen feet away, apparently following her scent trail. I sit on the ground and watch him and then decide to sprawl on my belly about four or five feet away, the better to take the snake's view of things.

He is a fat snake, and as he glides he slowly moves his head from side to side, tongue flicking, searching for scent. The air is still, the silence so total that the buzzing of a fly seems the only sound. He is alert and yet somehow relaxed as he wanders back and forth, nosing out the scent trail. Finally, after a good long spell, the male gets to within one or two feet of her. He coils on the opposite side of a log and rests. Later that afternoon he is in the same position, and again the next morning. I have brushed against snaketime, where even the imagined urgencies of mating follow protocols whose outlines we barely know. Fourteen days later, days spent together often within a foot of each other, they finally mate.

The color blue cost me six hundred dollars. I saw a stained glass lampshade in a shop. The shade had no pattern but what stopped my eye were jewel insets of a deep cobalt blue. With the base, a modern copy of an old style, I was out the money. Each evening I stand in our yard and see the glass glowing with color, especially the blue. It is not the blue of the sky or of a flower or of anything in my past life. It is the blue that blue should be and seldom is. I have become dependent upon the gleam of that blue in the early evening when I stand in the blackened yard and stare back into our home.

The color for me is a desire and desire for me is a real force and this force for me is not rational but something that precedes reason and tramples on it. Everything about snakes is explained rationally by using a utilitarian standard that insists whatever they do helps them to survive and reproduce. I do not believe this. It is not a full-time job being a blacktail rattlesnake. Blacktail rattlesnakes have a kind of time our kind seldom knows: free time. In free time, things do not have to be rational or irrational. They can simply be. Blacktail rattlesnakes, to our knowledge, do not have to explain themselves. We have to explain everything. We cannot simply be.

The scent of perfume, the flash of the eye, the feel of fabric, the blue glow off the stained glass lamp, all must be explained, do not exist to us without explanation. But imagine desire with no reckoning, imagine desire as headlong and not explicable. Imagine it is not explicable because no question is ever asked and thus there is nothing to explain.

What we know of blacktails is what we ask. In the thousands of observations made by Harry and Dave there are incidents that are not explained by current knowledge. But these incidents are already explained by the belief that they will be explained. Just as human psychology as practiced turns out to be a kind of relentless murder of human experience. But I retain my attraction to the blue light glowing in the night and I do not think the power of the glow comes from biography. Nor do I think the pleasure of that glow splashes over into utility. Perhaps form does not follow function. Perhaps at times form follows nothing at all but desire, and desire feeds off some swamp within life itself that cannot be mapped or charted or weighed or balanced.

I do not think everything can be explained, any more than I think my lifelong desire to be something else can be explained. But I know it is a fact and I cannot find any utility in this fact, even as I spend seasons with rattlesnakes, my belly to the ground, envying their slithering in the splotches of light and shadow along the creek bottom.

I have stood next to trees as lightning shattered them, walked into the wash to experience the flash flood storming toward my face, entered the cave and seen the lion's eyes glow in my beam of light, gone to the snakes, beaten myself all but to death in waterless desert marches. Gone to the mountains also. Ridden out storms on the lip of cliffs, let the riptide take me out to sea, sat company with the curious coyote that came to my camp, felt bats flutter along my flesh and explore my hide, watched a centipede amble across my bare chest. I cannot remember most of it but I can taste all of it and it is never enough.

Desire reaches past thought and escapes its strangling hold. I have no memory of acting impetuously. Thought seems to color my moves. There have been rough moments making hand grabs on cliffs when I could claim to escape the life of the mind, but such moments have been more calculated than my days in math class. Still, there linger moments of reaching and acting not so much without a thought as without the constraint of thought. That dance around a pool table when no shot can be missed. That sudden ramble on the first breeze of spring when all the old ground becomes new. The girls are in their summer clothes, the lake is warm enough for a swim, the garden is rank as I rip ripe tomatoes from the green stems. I slither on the ground following the snake, and I see everything with fresh eyes. And yet I feel myself constrained most of the time and can barely imagine a snake feeling that way. Perhaps this is what lives within the dream we have of the call of the wild.

For years I lived with a desert tortoise named Lightning. Early each November he went into his burrow and emerged the following spring. While he hibernated our yard seemed dead to me. For a spell I worked by a floor-to-ceiling window and Lightning would come over, get on his hind feet, and stare at me. Once in a while I put out plates of greens. Eventually I learned he had a savage hankering for bananas. I also learned that he reacted differently to different people. He'd follow me around like a dog as I worked in the garden. He liked the electrician and would paddle around after him as he worked. He hated the plumber, who always seemed to be digging up old pipes, and he would go underground for days once the plumber appeared on his turf. I never picked him up. I never made him into a pet. Once, a cat got into his food and he seemed enraged and chased the cat around in circles for more than a minute. He was my first bridge into what is called cold blood. I fell in love with a woman and he repeatedly charged her on sight—possibly, as one visiting herpetologist offered, as part of a mating drive. My woman concluded the tortoise and I had a homoerotic bond.

Beulah was a deeper current for me because I was afraid of her. I have no illusions about rattlesnake venom—a bite will not likely kill a healthy adult but the ride will be very rough and a visit to the hospital can run five to ten grand. And yet here I was whiling away days with a rattlesnake. I began to feel bad when company came and she disappeared, as if I were a thoughtless roommate.

I would slip into snaketime for hours, doing nothing as the snake beside me did nothing. It was not simply losing track of hours or days. It was diving deep into the moment and yet at the same time finding each moment immense and full.

We were cooking out on a ranch for an old friend sliding down the slope of cancer to his death. Thanksgiving had come upon him and he wanted to have kin in and to put on a feed for what he knew would be his last big wishbone. So they flocked in and we roasted two turkeys and made giblet gravy and dressing.

Just as I was taking the second turkey out of the oven to rest under foil as I made the gravy, the phone rang. Some dog had gotten into our yard back home and mauled our desert tortoise.

Our dog found him. It was thirty-seven degrees, he should have been underground in his burrow given the time of year and the temperature, but he'd dragged his bloody body down to the one patch of life-giving sun. Parts of his shell were gone, his beating heart exposed, the intestines in plain view. He didn't weigh a pound and was probably somewhere between five and eight years old. Tortoises, famously, can live a century.

By the time he recovered, months later, the bill ran to $974—intensive care, antibiotics, reconstructive surgery. He's ambling around our garden right now, eating cactus fruit, and so far as I can tell, swallowing ants whole.

But what I remember is the worried face on our dog, looking at him in that patch of light on the cold day, the pale sunlight dying toward winter solstice. And the drive to live roaring like a snare drum out of the mangled, horny hide that sought the patch of sun that, regardless of the condition, means yes.

Doesn't mean you will live.
Doesn't mean you will mean anything.

Doesn't mean there is meaning.
Means yes.

Harry Greene has spent three years figuring out how to ask a snake a question. The question is this: Do snakes manipulate their environment to their advantage? After Dave witnessed a blacktail in a hunting coil reach forward and bend down a plant that seemed to be blocking its view, Harry began to try to figure out how to ask this question.

He has some copperheads in his lab and he has three little bowls of water. One bowl has had a mouse dunked in it. Each day the bowls are rearranged. Each time the copperheads select the mouse-scented water they are rewarded with a mouse. So far, so good. They seem to be learning the game. Now he intends to put flimsy barriers around the bowl and see if they will bend them or alter them.

He is hoping against hope that he has learned enough to ask the snakes a sensible question. Such questioning is rather rare in the place we call science. It is a given that few animals use tools or do much of anything that suggests any kind of human cognition. We bank on this fact. We must keep the beasts at bay and in their place.

So we seldom ask them questions, lest they answer and terrify us by smashing our beliefs.

One June day about four A.M. I make coffee at the ranch, throw on a shirt, and paddle barefoot and bare-assed onto the porch to see the death of the morning stars. I feel something under my foot, hear a rattle and look down at Beulah, apparently on her way to the woodpile and a brief canvass for rats when she was arrested by my foot. I lift it and she slithers off.

That afternoon she is back at her post by the chair as I sit and read as if nothing had happened.

I have a pile of notes from Dave on the life histories of several blacktails. The snatches of behavior caught in the field form a kind of false history of months of calm punctuated by events—movement, denning, birthing, courting. Every time I string the notes into a biography I get the false speed characteristic of nature films, the montage of eating and fornicating and darting here and there. This montage misses the state of grace that covers what we cannot understand.

But of course, grace cannot be within the reach of snakes because it is a divine gift and snakes are beneath the cares of God. Or they are beyond grace because they are organisms with Latin names, locked within a logical schema of our own creation that bars God at the door. So I am left with the calm of the blacktails, the long silences and slow motion, the apparent lack of anxiety, the appetite that seems not linked to hunger as we know it, the courtship that is alien to our frenzied notions of love, the endless ribbons of time that seem a bower within which the snakes crawl and repose and live at peace. We are left with the fangs and venom and the strike, rare moments that reassure us of a kinship. We are left with these tiny seconds of violence as our strange comfort zone.

In the end, two things remain. Our knowledge of blacktail rattlesnakes is very slight. And no matter how much we learn of them, the fear never completely leaves. They do not hunt us, they have no apparent interest in us, they hardly ever harm us, certainly not nearly as much as we harm them. We can no more kill all of them than they can kill all of us. We are together in this thing called life. And they continue to baffle and fascinate us. This morning the male and female are still down by the creek, hardly a foot apart.

On an August morning, Harry's wife, Kelly, also a herpetologist, parks her truck about twenty miles from the study area in Skeleton Canyon in the Peloncillos and starts up the trail with one of her graduate students. She steps on a blacktail and hears the rattle at the same instant she is envenomated. An hour later her graduate student has her in Douglas, Arizona, where they administer antivenin and then medevac her to Tucson. Soon her badly swollen leg requires surgery. A runner who had been training for a marathon, she loses two-thirds of one muscle in her leg to necrosis, the death of tissue owing to the poison, and will eventually have three operations and months of therapy to restore the muscle and nerve in her leg. Sensation never entirely returns.

Nothing makes a person completely safe in rattlesnake country. Nor does anything make a snake completely safe. About three months earlier, a group of illegal Mexicans camped along the creek in the study area while awaiting their ride from a smuggler. Apparently they stumbled upon No. 26. Dave found the transmitter, with no remains. Harry speculates that they discovered the snake, killed it out of fear, and then ate it. Most likely it was No. 26's first and last confrontation with humans.

Near the anniversary of the bite, Kelly revisits the spot where she stepped on the blacktail. She begins to explain what she felt and then pauses. Finally she says, "I was surprised at the feelings I had."

And then she says nothing.

Few human beings are bitten by anything larger than an insect and only in some venomous reptiles is there a serious exchange of bodily fluids and the almost immediate sensation of being poisoned. Probably the only good-sized group of people in our society who understand this sensation are those in chemotherapy.

There is a soft eroticism in snakebites—the fangs, the injection, the sudden intimacy between two organisms—that stirs the embers of desire and fear that have created the legends of vampires. There is an easy overlay from the wilderness of Freud, where the snake is phallic, the act penetration. There is the notorious human fear of being devoured whole—anacondas have a global reputation even though few human beings have ever laid eyes on one. Lions rip us limb from limb yet retain our respect and affection. Snakes scare us to death. Not the actual snakes waiting in ambush out by the trail, but the much more real snakes embedded inside our minds. Field notes help knowledge to inch slowly forward but never get to the mystery of other blood and other forms of consciousness: the mouth, the fangs, the venom, the unblinking eye watching us from the tall grass by the faint rat trail.

I always think no rattlesnake wishes to bite me.

I always think the odds of being envenomated are slight.

I always think: I don't really care.

And I do not like to touch them.

The books are full of the fangs, how they fold down flat against the roof of the mouth until the scent arouses, the footfall rings like a bell, then the lunge forward, three and a half meters a second, the head sweeps upward, the fangs coming up at the flesh at a perfect ninety-degree angle, the puncture, compression of muscle to shoot out the venom, the tilt of the head as the fangs withdraw, the body returning to a coil in the flicker of an eye.

The options come now, cut a cross and suck, apply ice, don't apply ice, use compression, don't use compression, have special herbs, say certain words, carry a holy stone, pray, remain calm, have some bourbon, think about buying heavy boots for the future, all the options and still the poison spreads, pain comes, swelling, the heart races, and how far is it to help? On the shelf in the lab, remember the skull and fangs of that fer-de-lance, the bones light as air and the long special teeth floating before the eye like the dream of a saber, that luscious arc, such a fine point, the bones sleeping on the shelf now, safe and disengaged from the flesh, and the quick move, a state of grace that still stops the heart, not completely but in that first glance, yes then, stops the heart, causes a beat to be skipped. And then the music of life returns, the bones on the shelf are simply oddments of taxonomy, the serpents are names, Latin names, and special markings, little transmitters sending out signals from within their bodies, there, watch Dave dial one in, the pinging grows louder, it is very near, there, just three feet away, coiled and lost in some serenity denied us.

Before I go into the Australian outback, Harry says, Don't worry, you don't have to learn to identify the snakes there because they are all deadly. I park the rented car, walk out into the stark dirt, the emus standing and watching above the low brush, in the eucalyptus tree cockatoos screaming, a thousand miles north before my kind have safe streets again, and I look back at my lonely footprints in this big empty, not thinking of snakes because Harry was right, they are all deadly and there is nothing much to do but walk on, and the door opens, a torrent of sensation and form enters, the door closes and it is walled off again, the fangs fold back, the coil is resumed.

The rat trembles in the broken light along the creek. On one front shoulder there is a dribble of blood where the fangs hit seconds ago. The blacktail is very near and yet stranded on a distant shore. The poisoned rat apparently made a leap into a pile of brush after the strike, hopping from branch to branch. This exit has broken the scent trail and left large gaps of air for the snake to puzzle out. It is very hard to say how the rat is faring except to note that it will almost certainly die from the venom. Wild rats do have more resistance to the venom than laboratory rats. Perhaps life along the creek is a hopeless race between evolving rat resistance to the toxins and evolving toxins pouring through the fangs of snakes. Such thoughts open the creaking door of evolution and I briefly gaze into the cobwebbed workshop where change is relentless and yet painfully slow. I hold two thoughts simultaneously in my mind as I smell the lush summer growth along the creek bottom: evolution is a scientific fact, not just a theory, and the sun beating down upon my bare head will eventually die and be blackness in the sky. Neither fact means much to me, just as the law of gravity has the substance for me of a drunk-and-disorderly charge. What exists for me is a rat on the lip of doom and a snake on the lip of a late breakfast.

The snake moves patiently through the brush, tongue flicking, long body gliding as it goes up and down, disappears from view, and then returns, all the while slowly but with the grace and calm of God seeking out the scent trail of the rat. Over the course of half an hour the rat moves maybe ten feet away, the venom pounding its system, swelling its body, murdering its nerves and racing its tiny heart.

I suppose I should feel some sense of tragedy or some recoil from gore and slaughter. Instead, everything is sunlight, shadow, fresh green leaves, sweet air on the creek bottom, the pulse of life beating at something that feels like serenity. The rat is alone, the snake is alone, and all the clocks seem frozen in the midday light. I sit on the ground and watch the snake search. I have sought this moment all my life, the time when time stops, or at least moves hardly at all. The snake and the rat could be here waiting for a conclusion until the end of time. That is the feeling in my mind because in this small moment along the creek I have stepped outside of normal time, the thing recorded by the watch on the wrist, and moved into a different cadence, one so soft and soothing I lose all awareness of it. I cannot get out of my skin but I can, briefly, lose my sense of being imprisoned within it. The snake, a male numbered 46, slowly seeks its meal for thirty minutes. The next day, he has moved 120 feet and does not look to have the bulge of a rat in his body.

Two hours later, away from the creek up a side arroyo, male No. 28 is locked in a tail tangle with female No. 33. He is trying to coax her to open up her cloaca for intercourse. His body crawls on the top of her body, his head gently nudges down on her scales. She keeps softly moving away. No one is sure what the start-and-stop courtship means to snakes, and there are only the words of speculation that suggest she is testing to discover which male has the grit to father her progeny. Several of us are watching. The snakes pay no attention to us. Finally the male, perhaps struck by the shrinking shade as the sun glides westward, breaks off the encounter and slides uphill, then makes a 180-degree turn on a rock and slithers back downhill, where he disappears into a hole. This is unusual. Males in the literature do not give up courtship. After a few moments the female follows his scent trail and executes the same route before disappearing into the same hole.

No one knows exactly what this means. But then no one really knows much of meaning when it comes to blacktail rattlesnakes. We have our still images, our film, our notes. We can study them as reports from a foreign planet.

The rains finally came to the ranch in early July. The wash ran, the stock tanks filled, and the hills turned quickly green. At night thunder and lightning filled the valley, and one evening huge bolts shattered oaks and mesquite near the house. Beulah disappeared and I never saw her again. I assume she struck out into a new and friendly country, possibly for the courtship rituals that come with the summer rains. A friend moved into the ranch after I left. A rattlesnake, maybe Beulah for all I know, killed his dog near the house.

She could still be alive, patiently tasting the days and nights on the ranch. But mainly she lives inside my head, especially in the evening when I sit alone in the dark out in the yard and share the lessons she taught me of snaketime.

I make myself into the odd man out. I seek out cafés that do little business. On my first visit I will bring a book, sit in the corner, barely look at the menu, place my order, and avoid any conversation. I tip generously and after maybe two visits no one ever tries to talk with me and I no longer need to bring the book along.

Soon I am invisible, and that is when I cease to be alone. Just as I have learned to be still for the first three minutes in the presence of a blacktail rattlesnake, learned that I then also become invisible and am allowed to join the world of the rattlesnake.

The staff talks as if I do not exist, they sit in the corner, their bodies relaxed. I can glimpse the face of a woman and her entire life flashes on her skin, a series of headlines about men who left, cars that broke, children who rebelled, the dream of a pair of stylish shoes. The busboy shouts heavy metal, girls who scorn him, how a large engine in an old car with a highly polished body will change his life.

That is when I cease to feel alone. That is when I drink blood.

No, I am not a vampire, I am a person trying to break out of prison.

When I try to speak of these matters, I cause pained expressions. The younger people tell me it does not matter, the world is fucked. The older people tell me they do not wish to think of such things. The officials tell me I am crazy. I am left with the beasts, and others tell me they do not matter because they are dumb. Or I am left with the trees and grasses and bushes, and others tell me they cannot feel and are beneath notice.

I have never believed in the Garden of Eden except for the one I live in.

Nor have I believed in the Fall, even when I pick my bruised body off the ground.

As a boy, I rode a snake about the countryside and would tell my parents of my adventures. I have never lost this yen to cross over and be the other. Nor have I retained this sense of the other. It has been erased, worn away by the years.

Two things I can assert: There is no other. And the future has begun and fear of the future is of no value because it cannot be avoided, negotiated, rejected. Or embraced.

I do not want to understand the snake. I want to be the snake. And by this desire, perhaps even this act, I do not want to cease to be. I cling to my ego. I simply want to glide like a boat on the water into this other organism because I know that we share a common life and yet have different cultures. They are not like me but we are like each other.

I listen and I hear the beasts and plants must be cherished because they may be of some utility to humans. I listen and I hear they must be cherished because they are part of a web of life and this web is the safety net for humans. I cannot abide this talk.

It is blood for me.

I do not cherish the beasts, I enter their flesh. I do not guard the forest, I vanish into the deep wood.

I do not fear the cataclysm. The past is nothing but vast die-offs, violent weather, seas rising and receding, hot rocks falling from the sky and obliterating huge families of life.

What we fear has already happened and will happen again.

I drink my goblet of blood and feel the future rush down my throat.

There are three of them, and they are young and male. So far they have killed one hundred. No one knows what to make of their blood lust. True, they saw their families slaughtered and became orphans. But their rampage is without precedent.

They are three African elephants and they have murdered fifty-eight white rhinoceros and five black rhinos. They live in a game park in Africa. In another such reserve, young males have taken out forty rhinos and a number of their own kind. In the past, there is said to be almost no record of such violent behavior.

But something new is in the wind. I can taste it.

I drink my blood.

You will get the chance if you are open and live in love and not in fear. The day will surely come and you can go to the cave. You will know because you will hear music when the sun burns at midday. Then the door to the cave opens and you enter and they are there, two lines of them, and they are called Surem, the people before we became the people. They are short and they live in a world of peace and love, one we lost hold of when we put seeds in the ground and changed our ways.

You walk down the line and the Surem have gifts. You take what you need, a musical instrument, maybe a tool or some other item to help your spirit.

Of course, you say thank you and keep walking in the cave, walking and you get to the center of the place and there you find the gigantic snake. You are scared, the snake seems fierce but this is not the time for your fear and so you walk into its mouth.

Eventually you will come out.

A friend will tell you that you were in that snake for two weeks and you will be stunned because you thought it was but a day.

But this must not happen, this visit to the gigantic snake, this gifting of song wisdom by the Surem, until you are ready for such an experience. So do not go out in that desert at night, not until you are ready.

The people believe another thing. That in the long ago, serpents, huge serpents, came from the sea every seven years and they destroyed much, took down the houses, ruined the crops. But Suawaka, that one with intelligence, he would come down to protect us from unnatural creatures. Some nights you might see a big streak of light falling in the sky, not the path of a meteor but Suawaka coming to our aid. He is up there now, a being in space, watching the earth on our behalf.

These are two tales of the Yaqui, a desert people in my dry ground.

They are fables, of course, things that have no standing in our world.

But they are on the menu. And if you order them and swallow them, you will tear through that veil that hangs like a shroud and blows you from them.

Eventually we all must enter the gigantic snake. Or we will learn no music and our spirits will grow lean and blow away like ash from a cold fire.

Room

I think I'll make it through the night, thanks to the air conditioner roaring in the old motel. The drapes are pulled shut but a sliver of light slips through and plays across her body. I can smell her and hear the curious breathing, a deep inhale followed by a flutter of air, a kind of humming commentary when she exhales. The digital clock glows blood-red at two A.M. and I think I can also hear a hum coming off it, a faint tinny sound that cuts through the chuff chuff of the air conditioner. I do not think about the body on the morgue table.

Once, a local cop told me about a time he crossed the line to view a body in the morgue and found all the stiffs floating in a tub of something with big numbers marked on their backs. The attendant pulled his out with a hook, he said, like a fish for sale in the market. I listened and wondered, Is this too good to be true? And what was the smell like in that room? And was there this chuff chuff sound from an air conditioner? A hum coming off a clock?

That odd flutter in her breathing catches my attention and I put my hand on her thigh and then slide it between her legs where it is wet and warm and the short hairs brush against my fingers. I can tell she is awake though she does not stir. She'll be gone in a few hours. And I'll be back looking for one photograph of one body in that morgue over there, a body that now, thanks to the cop's story, floats in my mind in some tub with a big number on its back. The face will be twisted, the lips apart, and a silent scream will come from the throat. I want that silent scream, but most of the time I doubt its existence. It is more likely that nothing is lodged in the throat, not a scream, nor a sentence, just a brute silence as death descends. But still, I think, it would be odd to be recorded as having drowned and then to discover that one had been tossed into a tub with a number. Assuming such a tub even exists.

There must be a way to say yes and yet not base this yes off a life of no. There must be a way to say yes where you cross the river, face the corpse and stare into the dead eyes. Just as you accept the broken levee, the flooded and ruined city. The angry skies, the rising human numbers, and seas racing inland. The ice melting, also.

I think without the yes, there is nothing but lies and the ticking of the clock as we wait for the end of our time like a prisoner in a cell.

That is why the snakes matter to me, because of that yes. That is why the bite matters and the pain. And that is why I am here, in this room, looking for the dead.

And that is part of the problem: the room.

Is this where I gather the strength for yes? Or is this the tomb where I wait for no?

The elephant troubles me and I cannot figure out why. There is this small article off the wire about an elephant over there, across that line, a hungry elephant in a circus that cannot afford to feed the beast. So he grazes by the public highway far to the south in this other nation.

I think of the elephant constantly trying to eat, swallowing in a rush, in a desperate move at least to stay even.

I sniff the close stale air of the room and feel a weight on my chest.

Lately, the best part of my life is this pleasant darkness, the walk down the carpeted hall, key in the slot, then the door opens, the stringent air sagging with soap, bag down on the chair, quick footsteps to close the drapes, the blackness wraps around me, always the clock glowing by the bed, the menu for porn movies atop the television, an ashtray with one pack of matches, the strip of paper across the toilet seat, a stab at one fat button and then the chuff chuff groan of the air conditioner, a tinny blade of sound cutting through the white noise of the machine as it battles with its own internal parts, all this part of a ribbon of highway with every room along every route the same and the blackness the same and the air the same and the clock the same and the cable channels the same. I realize that this is the constant, the blackness, this is the firm and reassuring core, and everything else out there, the towns floating across the windshield, the pumps spewing gas, the bad coffee on the counters with sugar scattered, all that is faint, lacking substance, a thing to be raced through to get back to the room, the next room, the last room, all the rooms.

The job, the phone messages signaled by the small blinking light, the daily specials written on the whiteboards of the restaurants with grease pens, this I no longer believe in. I want to believe in them but somehow they have moved beyond reach. I have no word for my feelings. I am not alienated. I am not lost. I am not angry. There, that is it, a clot of nots, and somehow I cannot muster a single actual word to describe this sensation. I am not depressed, ah, there it is again, another claim of something I am not. Nor do I feel singular even when I sit in the room downstairs in all these motels where they have coffee, some rolls, the television always on to the news and I look at the other faces and see agendas and plans in their eyes, see goals and schemes, even then I do not feel singular. Because I know we all share one thing: we are all living underwater and yet we cannot get wet.

The room is the home, the place where my mind roams and is free. I think I no longer need maps in my nation because all the roads lead to the room and the room is always the same room, down to the air conditioner that sounds, always, as if it is on its last legs.

I am not on the road. There, again that *not.* But I am not on the road. I am moving and yet always in the same place.

I slide my hand down her leg. Her breathing continues its curious pace. I brush my lips against her mouth.

Her eyes open and she says, "Do you want to come on my face? You can, you know."

I stare straight ahead out the car window, my eyes glazing as the tiny stores drift past. I can taste the black exhaust of a city bus on my tongue.

The front of the restaurant mimics those seaside stalls on coastal beaches, the ones with palm fronds forming a roof and fish grilling and sea breezes wafting through. But beyond the fake front of this place in the heart of the city everything vanishes, the thrum of a million people goes away, and suddenly the world is windowless, the tables are solid, the waiters a flurry of attention. The money comes from an outlaw state to the south where the business flourishes. It is one of their places and it is designed to remind them of home.

A plate of food costs a day's wages. I order a bottle of wine and *camarones a la diablo.* The chips are fresh and smell of corn, the salsa a mélange of ground *chiltepins* in oil. I run my fingers over a tabletop of wood frozen in a crust of urethane. The room feels silent and I cannot hear the air conditioning unit. I glance to the back of the dining hall where four men sit at a booth, all with their hands below the table and probably clutching pistols between their legs. The deal. I snap a chip between my teeth, my tongue coming alive to the salt.

I first see her at the counter in the gas station. She is asking the girl at the register about her eye makeup. She is tall and big-boned and her hair hangs in two pigtails like a high school kid. The eyes say this is a lie. The girl at the register brightens and disappears into patter about eyeliner and whatnot. I watch the two guys move up and down the aisles stuffing chips and candy bars into their coats.

Outside I hear them laughing as they stand around an old car. The woman with the pigtails takes a deep drag on her cigarette and then they get in the car and melt back into the flow of the interstate.

The face glows a dark brown and a smile rockets across the round cheeks. He cannot sit still. The eyes are dark too, and the head keeps ducking as he speaks and he speaks very fast. He is flipping photos onto the saloon table, images he grabs like a fishmonger nabbing a cod off the shaved ice of a display case. He swallows some beer, plunks the glass down on the table, and never, not for an instant, do his hands stop moving. The air sags with smoke. The dull mirror on the back bar is submerged behind months of smoke, and the bartender never seems to look up. This is the place people come for a drink and then vanish forever. No one talks about this. The border is a few blocks away down the street, rich with sewage smells. A block off the avenue the throngs of whores begin, the streets dotted with taco stands that run day and night. This is basic geography for the man flipping the photos.

He briefly looks up and stares at the gringo sitting across from him, stares at me. The motel and the woman with her mouth open, that is another time right now. The negative is the thing, the simple little frame.

"Ah," he says, "yes, I was there, I got the shot." The body had bruises, duct tape held the hands together, and a big cord was around the neck. There were many signs of torture.

Yes, he saw it come out of the river, it was not a drowning, no, no, not that at all. He laughs at the memory, then drains his glass of beer, raises his hand to the waiter, *otra, otra,* and goes back to flipping through the photographs. He keeps them all in an old box, little slices of film crisscrossed with scratches, the prints torn and bent. Every once in a while the box gets stolen from his car, poof, his life's work gone, and then he gets another box and begins anew.

"But do not worry," he advises me. "The negative of the body is at my place, right there on the nightstand by the bed, we will get it in a while, no problem, here, have another drink."

The photographer has a room somewhere but the room keeps changing and everyone says he really lives in his car but the cars keep changing. He buys old junkers, runs them for a month or two or three, and then they stop running and he buys another. Many of the cars he buys are hot. He buys them in the barrios where the police do not show their faces.

I try to be patient, not to push. Pushing gets you nothing.

The woman who distracted the clerk in the store by the interstate while her companions stole snacks is certainly at work now, hitting the doors and smiling when someone opens, beginning to sell, her hair done in pigtails, the makeup understated, the pitch, so many points and she gets a scholarship for school. Her blouse has long sleeves, no tracks in view.

Sometimes I wonder about the birds. What do they think of us? The city is wind and the birds always seem to be fighting their way through the sky. Or the city is dust and the birds, I think, must choke in the brown sky. The city is sewage and I wonder if the birds get dysentery.

But mainly I wonder why they are here. They can fly away, go to some clean forest, listen to a mountain brook. The trees that used to line the avenues are all dead and gone. People no longer swim in the river. The people come because they have nowhere else to go. This is as far as they can get without crossing the border, the very edge of their cage.

But I wonder about the birds. Why do they stay?

The ground is brown, the little buttes line the river, the air cool in this high desert. A scrub of mesquite and creosote ripples in the wind. The dam backs up the river into a snake of a lake. All the major points have ancient names that everyone mispronounces.

I look out the truck window as the dull earth streams past.

After fifty miles of desert, a town breaks my peace. The killing was here. The man lived in a trailer, held a steady job. The neighbors said he was quiet, kept to himself. He lived with a woman but she hardly spoke. The first sign was a woman running naked down the dirt road wearing a dog collar. After the police arrested the man and his lady, they found the rack, the wires, and endless videotapes. They can't find most of the women recorded on the endless videotapes.

He was a quiet man. This is a quiet place. That is what everyone told the reporters.

The police think the man picked up the women at truck stops. No one missed them. Then he took them home.

I roll this around briefly in my mind, then let it slip away. I must hurry. The woman with pigtails is somewhere down the road ahead of me. I must get to the room, the same room that is always down the road, the drapes pulled, the air conditioner struggling, the dock glowing with the exact time.

I stretch and this lets the tightness out of my limbs. The truck is on cruise control, the music is blaring some blues, seventy-eight miles an hour, gas every three hundred miles. I can calculate my arrival down to the minute. I glance at the homes that stream past me in the towns.

Get to the room.

I have thought about the negative. That is why I am going back. I must have it. It will prove something. It will be exact, just like the room, exact, finite, with hard and real boundaries. I already know what happened, the drowning that was not a drowning. The autopsy reports that are a fraud. The look in the eyes, yes, that is it. The negative will give me the look in the eyes. Pain? Surprise? That is the part I do not know. If I get the negative, then I will know that look.

The matriarch is ill. She can't get up, so another matriarch comes over and lifts her to her feet with her tusks. But in a while she falls again, and this time she will not rise. She dies. Matriarchs from other families visit her. They stand over her giant body, their trunks delicately take in the air a foot or so above her. They nudge her carefully with their tusks.

We call this compassion. But of course we hesitate to say the word because we are speaking of elephants and we draw lines on the earth and we draw lines when it comes to other bloods.

I hear I am going there to see my father, I hear I am going there to meet my mother. They tell me I'm going over Jordan, been telling me since I was a child, those voices in the church where all I can smell is dust, the air full of it, gleaming spots of dust dancing in the sun as the tired words sing out and voices drink deep of hope, going to meet them both, over Jordan, and she says my Savior will be there but my father he says nothing of the sort, he just goes. And my God I have kneeled and used my tusks to raise them when they staggered, my father those last months, legs swinging out like a stork as he tried to stroll down the hall. My mother— *"Son! Help me"*—and I lift her from the bed, take her to the bathroom, wipe her, and we stagger back and the night rolls on. I know the elephants would understand as they sniff with their trunks, tusks gently reaching under to help the matriarch gain her feet and march toward one more sunrise. And the big ball of dirt spins and the flowers flood the air.

In the room there are always more things than elephants. That is why I check, position that digital clock, shut those drapes, hit the button on the air, light a smoke and wait for the visitors.

Other bloods, including the bloodless.

I answer the knock at the door, always.

I count to ten, slowly. Then I get up and cross the room and rub my fingers on the rough fabric of the drape. I nuzzle it and it smells of dust, smoke, and cleaning solvents. I open the patio door and my ears suck in the slow roar of the interstate. I close the door and hear the satisfying clunk as the lock engages. I think how easy it would be to shoot me as I stand here in front of the glass patio door. I think the glass is made from sand and the sand means beaches and the breakers are rolling in from across the Pacific, my skin will be red and hot from a day in the sun, the coconut scent of tanning oil, the salt dried in my hair, the moon rising over the bay, schoolgirls dressed in their summer clothes. I count to ten, again.

I am in the room and have reached my limit.

I can almost make out the face in the negative. The hair is dirty and lank, the jaws slack. The teeth? I lean forward but I cannot make out the teeth, not yet. I smell the chemicals from the tub, feel the hook slicing through the air. Hear the gurgle of the chemicals as the body turns and the number comes into view.

The man says, "I will take you there."

I think, Why not?

I know two things: I must have the negative and the negative does not exist. The negative never exists. It is the bait, the promise of knowing, just like the exact time glowing red on the clock by the motel bed. For years, when someone asked me the time, I always gave the exact time, down to the minute and second. I do this still, even though I do not own a watch, even though I never know the time, I do this because it comforts people, this knowing, this having everything exact.

We leave the bar, walk half a block, turn down a side street, get in the old car. The man gets behind the wheel, leans down, touches two wires, and we are off.

I know what comes next. In five minutes we pull into the parking lot of a beer store. A plastic bag, some crushed ice, six cans of Tecate.

We each open a beer, the man is happy now, beer floors his life. He is a good companion because he does not know fear. He has been beaten many times and he keeps photographs of his face after each beating. Nothing ever touches his smile.

He is on a mission, this Mexican. He is that rare man, one on a mission. He will get the picture with his camera. He does not know when or how but he will get it. The picture, he explains, and he explains this whenever he has had a great deal to drink, will be of his own death. The perfect picture. They will be coming at him with the knife or the gun. They will have duct tape to bind his hands and cover his mouth. They will have torture in their minds. They will outnumber him and be dreaming of placing him in a hole in the ground and perhaps burying him alive. They do this, you know. No matter. He will get the perfect picture, the image of his murder. He always smiles when he says this, the part about the picture as they kill him. The camera will record it on film, the negative will exist.

The camera? Maybe they will steal the camera and take the film out and destroy it. This does not matter because he will have the picture and a picture lasts but a little while anyway. But to have the picture is proof and to know is to win. To know is to exist. To not want the picture, to not want the negative is never to live. We both know this, believe this as we ride in the car through the city drinking beer. This is our secret. We know and others do not.

Once, the room was in a casino. Downstairs it was always day and night and all the times in between. One wall of the room was glass and looked out at the rows of casinos lining the main drag. The bathroom had a porthole so that when bathing, a person could look out at the living room. I never turned on the television, hardly ever went downstairs to the gambling. The first night, I drank a bottle of wine and then slept.

The second night, she came in by plane with another bottle of wine. I never turned on a light and we lived by the glow of the casino signs coming through the glass wall. I could make out the swimming pool far below but hardly anyone ever went there. I stretched out on the bed and watched her shower through the porthole. Her shoulders bent forward and she looked like a bird under a fountain. Her skin was very white, her hair short. The eyes anxious yet alarmingly clear, as if whatever her fears, she did not know how to lie to herself. She never finished sentences.

I listen to her drying herself, the soft rub of the thick casino towels against her soft body. She walks out of the bathroom and over the beige carpet to the huge bed. Her gait is small quick steps, the shoulders hunched, hands up next to her breasts, hands held exactly in the same way as scientific illustrators habitually portray two-legged dinosaurs in lush yet eerie landscapes. She slips in and sighs. I get up and strip off my clothes.

I pull her near me and she whispers into my ear, "I missed you."

As I hold her, I can feel her shudder. She smells of soap and I lick her ear. A spasm rocks through her and I hold her tightly. She is experiencing some kind of convulsion. But I say nothing, just as I never ask about the endless numbers of pills she is always swallowing.

"It will pass," she says.

I do not ask what is passing and she does not explain.

This night was unusual. After she came to bed and I got up to take off my clothes, I'd pulled the drapes shut, as always. But later I got up in the slow hours after midnight and pulled the drapes open. The casinos glowed silently through the thick glass. The casino signs seemed to demand that I open the drapes.

I check in and walk down the hall to my room. That is when I hear the voice, the sweet church voice. I look to my left, and a short fat man with a balding head is surrounded by a crowd of kids, scrubbed and clean-cut, sitting around on the floor and perching on the dresser. The man is giving orders, a daily pep talk to his sales force.

She is standing there with her pigtails, and she says, "Yeah, Stan, but just don't fuck with our happy hour."

I cannot tell exactly what they are selling.

I imagined meeting her in a bar hours later and buying her a drink. Triple vodka on the rocks. She will knock it back in an instant and I will order another.

I will tell her about having seen her at the gas station.

She will smile sweet as can be.

I will not ask her anything. I will know better than that.

She will ask for a cigarette.

And she will not ask me anything about myself.

But she will smile when I light her cigarette, her teeth are even and clean.

I imagine all this in an instant as I walk to my room.

I bought a leg of lamb and deboned it. The meat, dark red and sticky to the touch, lay on the board flat and cool. I minced some shallots and mixed them with black molasses and then poured it over the lamb. Next I grilled it until the flesh was medium rare. I cut slices about a half an inch thick and arranged them on a platter, with rice and carrots on the side. I felt better. I had done something from beginning to end. I especially enjoyed cutting the meat free from the bone and then flattening it on the slab. I needed these things, the touch, the smell, the cooking sounds.

I did not need to eat. It was never about that.

We are sitting in a small dive, a whorehouse on the edge of the city. The night breathes across the desert. The room smells of urine. The Mexican I am with insisted on coming here. Do not hurry, hurrying will only make everything take longer, I tell myself. I know this and oddly take pride in this knowing. I know all about time, I tell myself. I am the only white guy in the place but really there is hardly anyone there anyway. There is of course a bartender, two old guys with sandals at a small table, and three whores, one fat and old, the others young girls. The young girls come over and I buy them drinks.

We are sitting in the far corner, and it is dark there. It is always this way, the places vary, as do the towns, but this is a recurring thing, like a dream that keeps recurring. This time the dream is all about getting that negative. The windows of the bar have blinds and these blinds have never been opened. The beers are small, *chicas,* but the girls insist on whiskey which of course is not whiskey. No matter, it is part of the price. To get the negative, I must hang loose and buy whiskey that is not whiskey and ride around and forget time, and this is easy since I know the negative does not exist, the frame that holds the face with the eyes open and the body rich with torture marks, I know this does not exist. That is why I must have it. Another Mexican has told me the negative does not exist, has explained that I am being conned.

I believe him. Still, it hardly seems to matter to me. Because if I do not want it, if I do not seek the fabled negative, then I no longer care and there is nothing but the rooms and the glowing clock and the exact time. It is like the road, everything streaming past, the truck on cruise control, and none of it really there until a woman runs naked down the dirt lane with a dog collar around her neck and screams and screams, disturbing the peace and order. Plus, of course, that cache of videotapes with the faces of tortured women, faces no one can put a name to. I will simply give up too much, give up a belief in proof and hard facts, if I do not believe the negative exists.

In this recurring dream, a thing that actually happens again and again in various bad towns, the young Mexican girl by my side is warm and smells of perfume. I know it must be cheap perfume but still, she smells good. Her eyes are almonds, dark liner, the lips red, the face smooth and maybe sixteen or seventeen. She wears shorts and a halter top. Her breasts are small. Her hands have no rings, her teeth are even and white. The hair falls black on her shoulders and she presses against me.

I ask the girl where she is from and she says and then tells of her journey, the car that cost hundreds of pesos for a seat, the five days on the road with eight in the car, flat tires and radiator overheating, the excitement of coming north. Her face grows girlish as she talks of her family and the trip and the guy who came with her and left her soon after they arrived. She says she has no baby but I do not believe her. The darkness of the corner feels right.

The first minutes in the room are always good. The rough carpet under my feet. The bed looking taut and serene. The clock glowing and the time floating in the darkness. The drapes, of course, are open and I immediately pull them shut. I turn the fan of the air conditioner to exhaust.

I no longer check the pay-for-view offerings. There is never penetration, which is why I prefer cooking. When there is a small kitchenette, I will stay in the room for days. I cook but I hardly eat. Mainly I make perfect espresso in a small pot I carry.

The tiny red light on the phone may blink with messages but I usually ignore it. Everything falls away in the room except for the present, and this present has no past, none at all. I cannot even remember the past when I am in the room. The only catch, especially in newer motels, is that once a day I must get the electronic key renewed at the desk. I asked once about this and they explained that in one motel owned by the chain, a man lay dead in his bed for three days before anyone noticed. So the industry shifted to a new protocol. I regret this intrusion.

On the best nights I can no longer tell the difference between a noun and a verb. I have always been suspicious of the distinction between the organic and inorganic and so I take this meltdown of grammatical distinctions as a hopeful sign.

Evil never appears until I leave the room and see the sunny faces of others.

I get up in the night when she finally falls asleep for a while.

I sit at the table by the pulled drapes, the seep of light coming through the slit where they do not close completely. I light a cigarette and look at the glowing clock.

I have lost track. The truck has 180,711 miles. I lick this thought and feel the safety of its exactness. Everything else feels slippery. I am too old, I know that. Whatever my age, I am too old. I remember once being in a room looking out over a city, and that time, the woman was standing at the window with the pale electric glow of the streetlights playing over her. She was naked and her body outlined and her breasts hung down.

I asked, "Are you okay?"

And she said, "Oh, yeah." She paused and continued on. "You know, psychologists have found that in their own minds people always see themselves as about eighteen."

But I have always felt old, not tired but old, old with seeing things streaming past my eyes, old from listening because I seemed to sense what was about to be said. Old in my work, a work I cannot even describe to myself. Maybe old isn't the right word. Maybe I'd felt not surprised often enough.

I am not eighteen, not in my mind, not ever. And I am not what other people say I am. I reached out to the bedside table. Solid, yes, I'd thought, solid. The table helped.

The woman stayed there by the window looking out with the joy of a schoolgirl, standing there naked staring out at the night lights of a new city and talking to me softly but never turning toward me lest she lose her joy in the promise of all those lights.

Here is what I keep thinking, in all the rooms: What do you do once you know? Not what do you know, or how do you know, but what do you do once you know? Not how do you live or make a living, but this other thing. Once you know, you cease to have a résumé. Even your past becomes difficult to retain. I know the negative does not exist and I know I must have the negative.

There was this time, after we had fucked, and then she sat up in the bed, her back against the wall.

She started talking about a wolf, this wolf that goes everywhere with her. She'd be in a strange town, and she'd catch the wolf out of the corner of her eye, just a glimpse, this full-grown timber wolf, the eyes like fire, there, just off a ways, keeping an eye on her, watching over her. Sometimes in the night she'd wake up suddenly and feel the wolf, feel the breath of the wolf, and she was never afraid, not of the wolf. She knew the wolf would keep her safe. Once on the road, she gets out at an ice-cream stand, she's wearing a coat and nothing else, and she flashes her breasts, the Mohawk she's shaved along her pussy, a simple necklace and some earrings, opens the coat and flashes, must have been about sixty degrees, the rush as her nipples harden, just opens up to the world and out of the corner of her eye she catches the wolf, softly padding, keeping her safe. The sign over her head on the wall of the ice-cream stand says SMILE.

I am certain this happened. Somewhere, sometime, someone.

Sometimes, usually when the glowing clock says two or three A.M., I will come awake. I never rise or sit up in the bed. Sometimes I smoke a cigarette but that is all. This is stone time when everything is rock solid. I believe in the wolves then and also in the negatives. Things cease to be words. The air conditioner is always roaring and set to the coldest setting regardless of the time of year and independent of where I am. The room is always frigid.

I can smell July ground in an Iowa cornfield, hear tugs in the New York harbor, feel the crack of the bat in Wrigley Field, taste an Irish coffee in San Francisco as bay smells seep across the hills. The intricate patterns on expensive brassieres, the thin strand of thong disappearing between the cheeks of her ass flames with color. Birdsong from five thousand feet up on a mountain stream bounces off the walls. That is the stone time.

Once, I drove a Cadillac to Chicago. It was someone else's car and I was delivering it from the West Coast. I took the son of a friend along for the ride, a college kid out for an adventure. The kid talked about modern art for hours and I listened. Somewhere in Missouri, deep in the Ozarks, where chenille bedspreads for sale hang on clotheslines by the road, in that country of Bible radio and fried chicken, the kid opened the glove compartment looking for something and saw the gun. He quickly closed it and said nothing.

A bar flashes past with a simple sign of purple neon tubing, then the darkness of the desert returns. A Mexican is taking me somewhere but I do not care. You have to trust someone and that is the person who will betray you. No one else can. I know this and so I simply let things happen.

The Mexican pulls over and kills the lights. We get out and the desert sweeps in and drowns us with its darkness.

"Can you feel it?" the Mexican asks.

"Yes."

We are in the place where they dump the bodies.

They have been disappearing. Millions were around when I was born, now a few hundred thousand survive at best. I know elephants only from circuses and a few zoos. I have not been to a circus in decades and I hate zoos. Cages are not like the room, because the door cannot be opened at will.

Still, at times I think of elephants and I never think of their size, never consider that they are enormous. Nor do I think of them trampling people or raging about. I think of them brooding, large blots on a scene, brooding and yet keeping their thoughts to themselves. Elephants in my mind are always out of context, never fitting into a scene, a photograph, a street, or a highway. Maybe it is the fabled size. But more likely it is the sensuous curve of the trunk defying all the straight lines.

I have thought there would always be elephants, that somehow they would continue to roam in big herds. I could not imagine where this would occur beyond the word *Africa*, and Africa meant nothing but black people, lots of green, and space. I knew its outlines on a map but had no other sense of it. It was not the heart of darkness. It was not a mystery, it was simply space, green, and elephants.

I think that elephants would understand the room. Sometimes I think it is the place they always knew, what with that large memory and all that space for a brain in their large skulls. At times I think of being in the room in the dark with a cigarette glowing, just me and an elephant.

I think about the room and the importance of the room. Even though it is always the same room, still it is important. I think it is as close to home as I can get. The other places, they are lies. The ones lining the streets with mailboxes, flower beds, and driveways. Sometimes a fence and a neurotic dog pacing. Those places with their kitchens and soft chairs facing a television that is always on. I know better than to turn on the television in the room. That would destroy everything.

I was helping a dead man move. The guy had maybe a week or two left. I put a box of his stuff down by his chair and he leans over, his gut swollen with edema and his face yellow with jaundice. He rifles through it and fetches up a photograph.

"This is my son and his wife," he says.

He hands the photo over. It is one of those fake sepia prints. The son is wearing a long slicker, a cowboy hat, the gun in a holster. She is the tart, the gown low cut, hair blond, full breasts spilling out.

The dead man says, "He can't come. I didn't want to tell you about this because I'm ashamed. He got in some trouble. He's wearing one of those electronic anklets. They won't let him come."

We say nothing more to each other. That is the way it is on the safe streets with houses and their kitchens, the flower bed out front by the walk. The dead man sighs. Talking is an effort now.

The desert streaming by the window, cruise control on, and then the room, black with the clock glowing. That is better. More essential. Like the negative, like the perfect shot when they come to kill you. A burning house is also the right warm image.

I leave the dead man with his box of things. Outside, the sky is blue and the sun warm. I drive to the room. I think of the word *home*. The white picket fence. Once, an old man in Michigan told me, "If you think you own your home, well, then just stop paying taxes on it and see what happens."

I think about that from time to time, along with the sepia picture and the woman with the big smile and big breasts spilling out of her Old West costume. I think about the tug and rub of an electronic anklet keeping one close to home. I think of the negative, also.

I track her down with a Mexican. The tracking has taken three days and nights. We've gone to her home, a shack made out of loading pallets with no water or electricity. That was the first day.

She was gone and so were the kids. A stray yellow dog hung back a ways but did not bark or make a sound. The door was open and inside a sagging bed hid in one corner, a small, two-burner propane rig stood on a three-legged wooden table. Heaps of old clothes were piled around, and everything was dust.

The neighbors said her man drank too much and came home and beat her, they could hear the yelling. He tried to strangle her and somehow she got away and fled with the young boy and the girl. They did not know where she went. Her man was gone too. Drinking, they thought. A half block down the street a large portrait of the Virgin stared from the wall of a *tienda* with a small cluster of candles guttering in the wind at her feet.

I looked back at the open door of the house, caught the eye of the yellow dog in the dust.

I knew the hunger for a place where the walls are safe and the air is love and the grass is green, the pantry full and the woodpile never shrinks. The place where noise ceases and speech begins, where music thrums from the floorboards and birds sing in magical trees.

I knew this place was not a place. I knew this place was not a kitchen or a living room, not a garage or a backyard or a swimming pool or a relationship. I knew this was the fact of my time. I also knew that the wolf did not watch and protect. I had been opening the doors for years and the wolf was never at the door. That no matter what was done, the woman with the dog collar would run naked down the street screaming. That the face would look up from the negative and in the eyes might be pain or might be surprise but the face would look up and I must look into the face.

I once stayed with a woman for weeks. The rooms were perfect, kitchen scrubbed, incense in the air, every book in its place on the shelf, the sheets clean and sweet. Flowers in vases, all the clothes on hangers in the closet, the sink without a single dirty dish. Her hair perfect and mouth pert with lipstick, a dab of perfume behind the ear.

As I stand in the dirt street before the abandoned shack in the wind and dust, I can suddenly smell that other woman, her Mediterranean skin, see her bright eyes, taste her soft body molded with carefully selected panties and bras. I can remember making love to her in the bedroom on the second floor, the window staring into the upper limbs of a tree, remember her moans and fresh-scrubbed skin. And whenever she took a bath I had to be in the house or she did not feel safe.

I turn to the Mexican and say, "We must find her."

The negative that does not exist. The face staring up, the

body a canvas of torture. The woman who fled the house after her husband beat her and went for her throat, she is the ghost of the negative. The face is that of her son.

We had done a line of coke at the bar. That is how we met. The Vietnam Memorial was a couple of blocks away, and for some reason I thought of that as I sucked the line on the light wood bar top.

She was blond and loud and very sure of herself. I went to the room. The hotel was fine and she popped open the minibar and tore through a small bottle of wine and a can of nuts. She was a professional woman and carried an attache case even when barhopping. She wore a long coat and sensible heels. As soon as I closed the door, she plunged her tongue into my mouth. Then she plunked down the attache case.

Afterward, she talked about her ex and I could understand that, the need and the rhythm of her words. I did not listen but I could understand, I was used to it. I told her that I thought words had colors and she said nothing to this notion of mine.

Then she called her daughter while stretched out on the bed. That was what I could never understand.

She hadn't a clue about the room, I knew that clearly.

She gets up in the night and goes to the bathroom and I watch her carefully. I know she can feel my eyes on her. She slips back into the bed and I touch her breast as if it were a foreign object. Then my hand slides over to her other breast. She breathes in and out, that deep inhale and then the flutter of her exhale. I put my finger in her vagina, then put this finger in my mouth. I run my hand down her side and slide it under one buttock. Caress her stomach, bury my head in her hair, lick her ear. She says nothing.

I probe her mouth with my tongue and feel her tongue come alive and explore my mouth.

I get up and pull her to her feet. Still silence.

She walks over to the drapes and opens them. A weak light plays across the empty swimming pool of the old motel. She stands with her back to me. I do not move. Her ass is soft and serene in the pale light, her hips a curve in silhouette. I step toward her and nuzzle her neck. She leans forward and puts each hand against the glass of the patio doors. Her ass presses against me and I enter. She thrusts her ass against my hips, grinds, and now I can hear the breathing again. I slide my hands around her and first feel her breasts, then massage her vagina. Her hips keep rotating against me.

At first I am afraid she will say something, then I know better.

I feel that ache, the same one that comes to me by the abandoned house on the dirt street with the yellow dog watching me carefully. The same ache I felt when I looked into the sepia picture the dead man handed me. I know other people will say it is loneliness but this is not true. Loneliness is not in the room. That is why I come here. The room refuses loneliness and other easy words.

I pull out of her and turn her around and kiss her. Then I take her to the chair by the table and sit her down. She opens her mouth and I slide into her and her tongue races back and forth and I stroke her hair tenderly. We leave the drapes open.

I buy the plant at a nursery on impulse. It is a Lithops, a small button of tissue that looks like rock and uses this natural camouflage to protect itself from animals somewhere in the wastes of South Africa. I rub my fingers on the dark brown plant and to my surprise it is warm like flesh. The plant requires full sun and is sensitive to cold. I look at it, a button flat on the potting soil of a small nursery cup.

I take it to the room and stay inside for four days, drapes shut, lights out, except for the glow of the clock. I eat pasta that I make in the small kitchenette, pour sauce from a jar over it. But I eat very little. The phone never rings, since no one knows where I am. When I finally open the drapes, the lithop is two or three inches high, distended from a deep yearning for light. I throw it away. It is not good for the room.

The Mexican disappears, leaves me in bad cafés where flies crawl over everything. He'll be gone an hour or two and then he will return with more information. We develop a rhythm of looking and for two days we look, knock on doors, question strangers at taco stands, wander about. Once, we are trapped behind a bus in traffic and I taste the metallic black exhaust exploding out of the tailpipe of the bus like a sudden flower. We go to a barrio. A mud kiln for bricks has just been fired and a black cloud from the burning tires rises up high into the air.

We stop at a café. Outside is the phone booth where a cop was executed at eleven in the morning. He was making a call, his wife and daughter standing next to him when two men came up and shot him through the head. The women were untouched. They are sprawled over the body in the photograph a Mexican took, weeping, one of the women lifting her head up toward sky. The image is slightly out of focus and overexposed.

I lived for a while farther south on a cobblestone street in an old town. Everyone in the countryside was poor and the men from the sierra were very lean. They sometimes rode into town on horses but usually they walked. Out in the villages, the houses were mud and open to the breeze. One family became friends and when they came to town they would stop. I got to know the uncles, all five of them. Their niece was sixteen and a problem. She had a bright smile and quick eyes and a small body. She should be with a man, her uncles told me. I would go out to their place where wild figs grew.

The house was three small rooms with a breezeway between them, but the family, eight or nine of them, really lived under the ramada. Once, I sat there in the dark and ate venison stew and drank beer while the uncles complained about their niece, how she should be moving on.

On weekends she would come to my house to shower before she went to the dance. I was very careful with her. I would move out into the yard as she bathed. Her uncles were disappointed, I could tell. They gave her money for these fiestas in the hope she would find a man to feed her. For a while she went off with a man who delivered corn chips in a small truck to the little store in her village. But after two weeks he brought her back, just dropped her off in the dirt road of the village and drove off without a word.

Once, I took a photograph of her. She accepted it with wonder and brought me a small carving of an elephant sculpted from the root of a cottonwood tree.

She would always stand close to me.

Whenever she left for the dance, she would wear high heels that she had carried into town in a paper sack. I would watch her move nimbly down the cobblestone street, her small thin hips swaying.

She makes me hungry and she knows it. We are on the bed. The glowing clock says it is three A.M. I am inside her. She takes my hands and puts them on her throat. I slowly tighten my grip and her tongue thrashes in my mouth. Then I take one of my hands off her throat and put it on her breast.

"Squeeze my nipple hard," she whispers. Then her tongue is back in my mouth.

The drapes are still open and I resent the light, the intrusion of out there into here. I feel the room may slip away.

We are having a cigarette now. Somehow, there has been a pause. The sheets are wet with sweat and the alcohol has poured out of our bodies and now we are calm but wide alert.

I want to lick her, to feel her hair against my tongue, but first I smoke. We exhale slowly.

I get up and close the drapes, the blackness comes back and fills the room with comfort. I slide back into bed beside her, gently take a strand of her long hair and brush it against my lips.

She starts talking. She is traveling in an old car with two guys. The car is black and rusted out from salt on winter roads. They crash in a cheap motel, a room with two beds. She gets into bed with one guy and they fuck. She can tell from the other guy's breathing that he is awake, listening in the blackness of the room. When she finishes with the guy, she just lies there awhile. The room is simply the sound of air coming in through the exhaust fan. Outside it is raining, she remembers the rain against the window. The guy beside her is limp now, she runs her finger over his fallen cock. She lights a cigarette and has a smoke, she remembers that also, the long exhale on the cigarette, the smoke rolling off her tongue.

Then she gets up and slides into bed with the other guy.

That is all she says.

I say nothing. The drapes are shut. I am okay for the moment.

I will go after the negative later. The image will have scratches, of course, but still the face will look up and I will finally see what it says.

She says, "We are like two whales singing from opposite sides of an ocean."

I do not touch that remark at all. I know better than to go there.

There is always this moment in the night in the room when I know. I can only seem to know in the room and I have ceased wondering why.

I will know what people say before they say it. I will know what happened before time and what happens after time. I will know what a rock thinks.

I will know what I will see in the negative. Know absolutely and savor the knowing. The case is closed. But it is not closed.

I can never stop wanting the negative.

We get out of the car and wade through some young toughs. We walk through a small store, then into a backroom, and then the room behind the backroom. She is sitting on a bed and her large eyes are flooded with fear. The Mexican speaks to her and we sit down.

She is thirtysomething and her face is very tired. For days, she explains, she has been moving through the barrios so that her man will not find her. When she speaks, she looks down at the floor. Her skin is dark, the body stocky.

They came for her son, she explains, and took him away. The police. When they brought him back hours later he had been beaten. Then, three weeks after that, some boys came to her door and said her son had drowned trying to cross the river. She did not see the body, she continues, but her sister did. And her sister said his head was caved in, the throat seemed to show marks of strangulation. No, she did not see this herself, she sent her sister to look at the body and decide if it was her son.

Everything is floating away. The small house where we talk seems to be the only anchor. The cement floor a dark red, the blond table in the corner holds a small television that silently flickers as she speaks. Her face is smooth and round, the black hair cropped and forming bangs over her wary eyes. She wears a faded blue skirt and yellow blouse, her feet dirty in plastic sandals. Huge pink earrings shout her hopes. The children hold back from her and stare with round eyes and unsmiling lips. Over her shoulder on the wall a poster of a beach with blue ocean water whispers space and warmth. A curtain hangs at the door and is tied aside. Outside, nothing grows in a dirt yard. Two men stand there around a fire and glance furtively into the room where the woman speaks. She talks hurriedly but softly and with no inflection. She is the mother who did not look into her son's coffin. Her head stays down as she speaks into the red cement floor. The air smells of grease.

Her younger son, maybe eight or nine, comes over, and she hands him a few pesos and tells him to go fetch milk and cereal. Her children have not eaten today. Her breasts ride on her chest as if asleep. She sits with her legs spread apart as if this helps her breathe.

We know that when we leave she will disappear and we will not find her as easily again. If we could find her this time, well, then she has not moved carefully enough.

Her toenails are painted red.

As she speaks, she pauses from time to time to scratch herself. Her skin is brown yet somehow fading as she speaks. Soon she will have no color.

The gun lies on the table. The table is round and has two chairs, even though no one comes to the room. I wonder why I carry the gun, a chrome-plated .357 magnum with hollow-tipped bullets. I feel neutral about guns but I hate noise, especially the roar and acrid smoke that comes from firing one.

Life is getting thin, and I can feel the thinness. The richness I usually find in the room is absent. Now all the verb tenses are here, the past, the present, the probable future. The gun, I think, has done this. It means caring about the future and that is where it violates the room.

I think of putting the gun in my mouth, just to feel the cold metal.

The negative floats in the blackness, the river rushes past

and the waters cleanse me, rinse every pore, and the face comes floating up, gently riding on the chemicals of the tub.

I am alone in a hotel bar. Three men in T-shirts with automatic pistols shoved into their pants watch me from the bar. I have my notebook out and my pen with black ink and a fine point. I am fussy about pens, they must be cheap and yet roll easily across the paper. The words must feel fluid. It is afternoon and a weak light comes through the small windows of the bar. The police come here also but they seldom wear uniforms and look exactly like the thugs at the bar.

On my table is a plate of melted cheese and some chips. I do not eat.

The trick is to not answer the question. The trick is to know that answers are lies. The boy was taken from the mother and tortured for hours and then returned. Later, he was said to have drowned in the river. The body showed signs of torture and the garroting of murder. The official autopsy says drowning. The authorities insist it was a drowning and become angry when questions are asked about this conclusion.

I bite into some of the cheese and all I taste is salt. I sip some of the wine but all I taste is vinegar. I try to recall her taste and can only come up with her scent. I can hear that flutter of air as she exhales. I light a cigarette and the bloom of smoke pouring from my mouth hangs in the still air of the bar. I look over at the thugs, who glare back. I sense a clock ticking, and unlike the clock in the room, the one that glows, this one tells a different time, a hard and real time. I have an hour or two. After that if I remain here, someone will move.

But the negative. I must deal with the negative, the one I seek that does not exist. There is a point, and I am at it, where biography is said to be essential, where some day or night in my life must be brought into view to explain how I came to sit in this bar with a pad and pen before me. A woman runs down the dirt road and she is naked and screams and screams and she wears a dog collar. There is a negative, the one that does not exist.

The room is empty when I return. The bed has been made, the room cleaned. I have been penetrated and the smell of solvents is heavy in the air. All the towels are fresh.

I sit down at the table, light a cigarette. I watch the exhaled smoke float away without a flutter. I realize the cleaning woman turned off the air conditioner. I must pull myself back together. I hit the button for the exhaust fan, pull the drapes shut with force. Now there is nothing but the glowing clock face and the red tip of my smoke.

The thing is almost spent, the hunt for the negative. I know this. I think I will give it one more shot.

That afternoon I wind up in a cheap café with a reporter. The guy also says he has seen the body and he describes it pretty much the way the mother did and pretty much the way the one Mexican claimed it looked in his fabled negative. Strangled, tortured, hands bound. The reporter has a goatee, a clipped and exact speech, and he pretends to make eye contact but fakes it, does that public speaker's trick of looking slightly above the eyes of the audience and thus wooing them while ignoring them. I watch the eyes not watch me and listen to the crisp litany of some moment in the morgue when the body is on a table, a stainless steel table, the gratuitous detail flung out to convince. I love these touches, these instruments of fraud, the care they indicate, the sheer love the other person demonstrates in pushing a version of events. And I enjoy the offhandedness of the conversation, the way the man with the goatee almost shrugs. "That body? The boy they said was drowned? Ah, him, yes, saw him on the table, clearly tortured and then executed."

"Did you publish anything about it?"

"No, why?"

And then the waitress comes by and pours more coffee and the moment passes, a little nonevent shared with me but of no consequence. So I sip my coffee and think that now there are three versions, a negative, a reporter, the mother, and they all agree on one fact, that the death was murder, not drowning. But what I enjoy most of all is that I know that the reporter is lying. Know that his eyes pretending to make contact give him away. That he never saw the body, that the detail of the stainless steel table gives away his tale. That he heard something, knows something, that is true. And his story may be true. But he was never there, not at all, and that is why he must fling out this one little detail of the table, to make sure he sounds as if he were there.

Now I sit back in the room, later, much later, and I exhale and the air conditioner is on and moaning and the reporter's tale and the thugs in the bar float before my eyes in the darkness and they are pure here, isolated images like figures a child cuts out of magazines with scissors and pastes on blank paper, now just so many details or incidents or anecdotes, scrubbed clean of deceit and violence and the smell of a body floating in a tub of chemicals, a body with a number written on its back. In the room with the glowing clock, all this mishmash of life can become that ultimate safe thing: a story. Something with a beginning, a middle, an end, pages typed out and then stapled together and put into a folder and filed in a drawer. Dust will slowly collect on the file case where the folder rests, time will pass. Peace will descend.

But none of this helps me. None of this explains to me why I remember a drowning that is a murder and why I want a negative that does not exist.

I snuff out the cigarette. I am glad that I do not want a drink. This means some deeper steadiness in me. I get up and go into the bathroom, pull the plastic wrap from a glass, and fill it with water from the faucet. The taste is chemical but the water is cool and it eases my mouth. I put the glass down in the darkness and feel satisfaction from the clink as it hits the enamel of the washbasin. So much depends on the clink of the empty glass on the white enamel in the dark room.

I like the fact that they are capable of crime. Tyke went crazy in Honolulu and murdered her trainer, then ran wild in the streets and was shot down. It required fifty-seven rounds to take her out. Janet lost it in Palm Bay, Florida, and was dispatched.

Experts say elephants have three basic needs. Food is a big one, and elephants can eat up to twenty hours a day. They need friends too, and form lifelong ties. Finally, they must have freedom. When confined, chained, and hustled about in stunts, they are prone to mental illness.

I never find any real stuff on this mental illness, a clinical description or the record of a session with a deeply troubled elephant.

There is this other woman.

Once, she sat up in bed and said, "The taste of cum really varies in men."

And then this statement floated away, a feathery thing blowing in the wind. Dandelions when they go to seed float away the same way, physically there and yet ghostly all the same.

Once, she mentioned organizing, going door-to-door pulling the poor out of the Mad Dog 20/20 and shadows. The poor in this fragment have no race. The cause they are being organized for never is mentioned. The time when this happens is also skipped. She does not smile when these historical moments pop out of her mouth but then she seldom smiles. Once, I took my fingers and touched her face and made her smile. When I took the fingers away, the smile remained. But she looked as if this act caused her pain.

I did not do it again.

She was short, maybe five feet. She moved quickly, always in a hurry, even if crossing the room to put more blues on. And she bent forward as she moved, with her there was always a wind blowing. Her speech was fast also and this clashed with a lingering southern accent. I could see her as a child with a torn dress and dirty face watching the traffic roar by on some blue highway. She had hundreds of blues, but she never spoke of the music, just played it constantly. Just as she never spoke of the drugs her doctor gave her, and maybe this was fair since they seemed to have little effect. She was always tense, her body coiled, even sprawled on the bed postcoital.

I thought of her from time to time when I was in the room. She always wanted to travel with me but I knew that would be fatal. In a way, it might be good, like a small suitcase I could pack and open whenever I wanted a fuck. But I knew more would come billowing out of the suitcase and I knew I could not control such episodes any more than she could.

She was the first woman I had known in years who wore white panties.

"I got on the bus the morning after high school graduation," she once said. No location, no date. A small seventeen-year-old on a bus leaving somewhere and something.

She was never secretive, she simply had no past to haul out when asked. Only these glass shards in her brain.

I sensed abuse, some kind of abuse. She was difficult about where to have lunch, testy on almost any issue or decision. And totally compliant in bed, like a wind-up doll with rubber limbs.

Once, in the shower, she asked, "Can I wash your back? That is my thing."

The only request, ever.

She was always angry.

"He was late," she said, "as usual, the fucker was always

late, and he never could get anything done, not even taking out the garbage, he talked too much and didn't do a fucking thing, just his organizing and that was nothing, Jesus H. Christ *I was the one down there making sure the files were in order and keeping track of everything*," and here she paused to sip some wine, even though wine was not her drink, she tended toward whiskey, one of those women with half-gallon jugs shoved in the cupboard out of sight. I was never around then, and maybe that was part of it, my not being around, and she'd drink for a day or two, binge, and then start calling and leaving obscene messages. Once, I got a single-sentence letter in the mail, a letter with no return address, that said "I wouldn't fuck you if you were the last man on earth." And then two days later a knock and she walks in and starts shedding her clothes, down to the white panties.

Anyway, she is talking about some guy, maybe someone she met when she got off that bus with her suitcase, he is coming in the door "and he's pretending like he is not hours late, and I've cooked supper, some meatloaf and potatoes and a nice salad, the fucking salad is all wilted now, and I'm furious and what does he want? He shrugs off everything, acts la-di-da like nothing has happened, and he wants a blowjob. He tasted bad."

I cannot remember a single memory knifing out of her mouth that had the scent of love. Not a single candlelit dinner, not a sunset rich with color, not a spring flower, not a night in a perfect bed in a perfect hotel with excellent room service.

Her mother was in the crazy place. So was a sister. Another sister had killed herself.

I came back once from weeks in the room. Walked through the door, picked the mail up off the floor. Found all the windows facing the yard painted over, the paint still fresh and wet. I never asked.

She was depressed.

Various men fell out of her mouth, a laundry list, but not the way other women talk about their ex-boyfriends and husbands, not a review of how they have been wronged. It was simply a history of assholes who had crossed her path. She kept her eyes open in bed, always.

I lie back on her couch. Dinner is over. I have taken off my shoes, the curtains are pulled shut, the blues fill the air. She walks over, leans down, and rubs my cock through my trousers. Then she opens my fly and sucks on me. Then she swings over me, her eyes glistening, her mouth not smiling but the lips slightly apart, her hair hanging down around her face. I can hear her breathing. She pulls up her skirt as if she were barefoot in a torn dress in the South and about to squat and urinate. This movement always has that same offhand quality. She is not wearing panties and her snatch briefly dances before my eyes. Then she lowers, takes in my cock, and begins to rock. The skirt drops and she looks at the ceiling.

After a while I pull her off and she sucks my cock as I shed my pants and shirt. Then we walk back to the bedroom and I sit on the edge of the bed while she undresses before the mirror on the dresser. She always turns away when she is naked, puts both hands on the dresser top and stares into the mirror, and I enter her from the back.

Later, of course, we shower and she scrubs my back. She likes to talk in the shower, almost as if she were catching up for her silence in the bedroom.

She seems like a natural for the room. But I never bring her, not once. I know it would not be safe.

The Mexican has that look of weariness with me. Not fatigue from too much work, not even boredom, but the weariness that comes from dealing with someone who refuses to understand the obvious and in that refusal threatens the few hard facts that, like pebbles, rub against the feet and remind one that there is a real world and that it will not go away and cannot really be known. It simply is, unchanging, unkind, and defiant.

We will be talking, say over a cup of coffee in a café or cracking some beers in the beat-up old car as it bounces through the potholes of the city's streets, and we'll be talking about the drowning that is really only a way to cover a murder, and I will return to the negative I want and to all the troublesome details and facts of the death, and then, out of the blue, the Mexican will start spouting the official version, rattling on about the autopsy report that a doctor has signed that insists the case is simply a drowning, about the police investigation that found nothing amiss, and so forth. Suddenly all the lies of the government are presented by the Mexican as facts, and all the corruption on the faces of the officials is erased and they are paraded before me as dutiful public servants. This always sends me spinning through space, this retreat to a vision of order.

Sometimes I systematically demolish these fantasies, roll out facts like a hanging judge at the moment of sentencing, and this act is like slapping the Mexican in the face, slapping him when his hands are tied.

My voice begins to rise and I strike words like keys on a piano. I say, "Wait a minute. Remember that day we crossed the river? We went to the fire station where the body was said to have been pulled out by their people. And the firemen not only denied doing this, they said they stood on the bank of the river and watched the Mexicans pull out the body. Then we went to the headquarters of the fire department and they checked their computers for that day and said they never had the body, and then they printed out the computer records for that day which noted they never got the body but watched the Mexicans pull it out. And then we went to the gringo doctor who was the county coroner and we met him in his office and he checked his own records for floaters pulled from the river that he carved up and reported on, and the boy was not one of them. Christ, I can tell you the exact location of his office, and how his door opened north onto a corridor and how his fucking desk was on the south side of the room and he was fat and balding and nervous about us and he never smiled and how he looked at us with hostility because he thought we must be after something but he could not figure out what it was. And of course, what we were after did not exist, since we wanted reports from his side which did not exist, because the body had never landed on his side. And you were there and afterward we went to that Mexican American joint and you had two Budweisers and I had a glass of wine and dammit I can draw a sketch of our table and where it was located in that restaurant and if you want to cross the fucking bridge I can take you to that goddamn restaurant right now. And then we went back to the Mexican consulate and they insisted, no, no, the body was fished out by the Americans and they gave us that Mexican autopsy report that insisted on this same scenario, the report that said the kid drowned and was not murdered. And after that we chased down the mother who told of the damage to the body. And she told us of the police visits and how they beat and tortured her son. These are all facts you fucking witnessed."

I stop talking, spent like a wind that has passed through and is now no more.

I go back to the room.

Someone has held hearings on the plight of captive elephants. There is testimony that they must be tortured in order to do the things that delight children and interest adults. One witness says, "Is it any wonder that these tragic captive elephants ... deprived of any semblance of the life intended for them by nature ... mercilessly beaten, some of them daily, to force them to perform ridiculous tricks ... robbed of every shred of dignity . . . Is it any wonder that these magnificent highly intelligent creatures finally rebel?"

Of course, everyone agrees that captive elephants live longer than free elephants. There seems no debate on this point. They just seem to lose their minds.

Or do they, I wonder. Is the rampage a sign of mental illness?

Zoo people argue that elephants are not mean, just fearless. An African male can weigh in at 16,000 pounds, a female at 8,000 pounds. People may muster 200 pounds. The elephants are intelligent. They know we are puny and they are big.

There are said to be somewhere between seven hundred and nine hundred people in my nation who work with elephants. One of them is killed each year. And no one knows exactly how to discipline an elephant, short of killing. They go unpunished or they are slaughtered.

I think they know they cannot lose even when they realize they will be killed.

The machine blows freezing air into the room. The clock faithfully glows. The sheets are clean and the bed still made. I sit in the chair by the round table. Once in a while I hear footsteps down the corridor and low voices as the late arrivals drag their bags. These days, the bags all have tiny wheels that seem to catch on every bump in the building's hallways. Sometimes I can hear what sounds like grunts and always there is the click of a key in the lock as metal touches metal and then the harsh shutting of the door. By this hour the televisions are pretty much off, except in the rooms taken by drunks, where the sets play very loudly.

From time to time I pad down the hallway to the ice machine and refresh my bucket.

The boy is dead, floating in the river, or floating in that tub in the morgue, or floating up from the surface of the negative. The only things in the room are the glowing face of the clock and the boy's face drifting in the blackness. I pull a cigarette from the pack, tap it on the table, and pick up my lighter. I hesitate. The flame will scar the room, I think. But I do it anyway, closing my eyes while I light the cigarette. The lighter clicks off, I open my eyes, and there is the clock, the red tip of the smoke. And the floating face. The face comes near and then recedes and this movement is based on my inhalations. Slowly, I get the sense of being a kind of accordion, squeezing light in and out, the face coming and going.

The boy, I know, was a petty thief and a coward, a follower and not a leader. He was none too bright. Every description has him hanging back. He is someone things happen to, a passive voice, not someone who makes things happen. Not once while he walked the earth.

I keep coming back to the negative and I come back to it since it will prove the boy was murdered. I have to cling to the negative, even though it does not exist. The negative, I realize, is my crutch, the thing that keeps me from falling down there. And what is down there? What do I hit if I fall?

Here I stop.

I have thought about this matter before but I have always moved on before the thinking got too hard. I go to the room, I leave the room, and then I return to the room. If I am not careful, I will fall off the edge of the world and be spinning in some blackness that is darker than the room. There is a limit to how far I can go.

Once, as a boy, I climbed into the attic at my aunt's farm. The day was bright and sun seeped through the small window in the dust under the eaves, where all kinds of chests and broken tables and rotting books had found their way. There was no real flooring, just the beams racing from wall to wall, and I had to be careful of my steps lest I crash through the ceilings of the bedrooms just below. I had never been there before and I felt a mild excitement. I was at the age when ghosts and unnameable things still existed for me. I rifled through the objects, looking for something solid, perhaps an old pocketknife I could rescue or, better yet, a long-forgotten gun that I could oil and reactivate. I loved killing things then, and regularly prowled the fields plinking at rabbits. I dreamed of luring crows in close and had saved my allowance to buy a call. Crows were adversaries, creatures much storied in the region for their cunning and thefts. Once, an uncle shot a crow and hung the carcass from the apple tree as a warning to others about any further filching of the ripe fruit. But I never could get close to the crows, and no matter how ardently I called, I could never seduce them into moving within range of my gun.

I pulled down an album off a dusty dresser, the cover a faded maroon. I idly opened it and started scanning the old photographs, noticing ancient cars in some of the shots, and unknown faces. Now and then I could make out the likeness of some relative but this was difficult because the faces were so much younger. Then I flipped a page and one image got my attention. The man was on the grass, and by his side was a woman. The man was my father, I was sure of it, my father with a different color in his hair, my father with a flat stomach and no creases in his face. The woman was young also, with short hair and a housedress, and she stared unsmiling at the camera. There was nothing in the background but more grass and some blur of trees. My father and the woman did not touch, but they were near each other on the grass. I knew instantly they were man and wife but that the woman was not my mother, nor had I ever heard any mention of such a woman. But I knew, could feel it rippling through my body. There was a carnality in the photograph even though the man and the woman were not touching, even though I did not know the word *carnality* then. Still, I could feel this sensation of touching, of being together. I knew the man and the woman in the photograph preceded my world of a father and a mother and somehow undermined it, refuted it. The woman looked thin, I remember that, and my father looked careworn, not at ease, but consumed by something. I never mentioned the photograph to anyone. Not to my aunt, nor to my parents. I cannot explain this silence, I just knew it was not to be mentioned. Twenty years would pass before the world in the photograph found words in my life. My father finally told me a little. He could not fix it. She eventually died. He had always been ashamed of it all, ashamed of his failure. He said no more.

That photograph now floats in the room along with the negative of the dead boy. It looks just the way a print does in the chemical tray of a darkroom, a tangible object slowly emerging beneath the fluid, visible but not completely visible, a thing slowly swirling into view but never quite getting there.

The negative floats and it is wet and the face comes nearer and nearer. I used to think a simple thought: that there were two worlds. One was the official world, the place talked about in pulpits and magazines and on television, the talk of it all in a code that a person had to learn but once learned, it reinforced the existence of this official world with every coded word and by that act felt safe and died in the same instant. Then there was the other world of violence and shame and whores and drink and crime that was the real world.

I have long since abandoned these distinctions.

There is just one world. In this one world, fluids flow, a protoplasm that glows in the dark, a surge of energy flaming through the black air. And yet these acts violate no time, require no stopwatch, have no beginning and no end, are never young, never grow old. There is no good side of town, and the trains neither run on time nor run at all. I hear this world in music, though not often. And I hear it in the silence between the notes. I see it in the white spaces that drench Japanese drawings. Sometimes I hear it in the moments when I do not speak, not even in the quiet of my mind. Once, I touched a woman's breast and could hear what she was thinking, hear clearly and understand her completely even though I could not make out a single word. And as I moved my hand I could hear her listening to me, and then hear her answer back in a regular call-and-response, hear her cries like amens in a church service. We did not speak of it afterward.

Coming closer, the face gaining features, the throat almost ready to speak, the sound lush and free of words, the hands bound with duct tape, the cord around the neck. One world, and the autopsies are of no matter.

I like the fact that they will not go down. That they stay alert and face whatever they must face. When an elephant goes berserk, two drugs are suggested to calm them, carfentanil and etorphine, both narcotics, both lethal in even trace amounts in humans. To calm an elephant takes a dosage of about ten thousand times a hit of morphine and a wait of eight to twelve minutes. The alternative is a round from a .458 magnum.

I know I would prefer the drug. First there is the sense of colors. Then of course the great serenity that comes from the spike. The magnum round would be swifter, but I hate noise. And the tearing of the flesh followed by the wave of shock cannot be pleasant. Hormones and adrenaline could counterattack this for a while, but still, the bullet is slow and not serene. I cannot get around this fact.

But I must consider, and I do consider, the pleasure of action. Of tusk goring a body, a foot crushing a skull, a trunk heaving someone over a wall. This satisfaction cannot be a small thing. I know this. I am attracted to these thoughts.

I want to think that deep in the elephant's memory there is a negative, some image or scene, that in the night comes floating up. The elephant neither wills this image nor avoids it. The elephant, and I think this when I am alone in the room after midnight, the elephant is like me, four legs to be sure, and that odd nose, but still like me, letting the image come, refusing to play safe, gliding as if on skates to the rim called the berserk.

People think that elephants make deep sounds that can travel for miles through the forest, sounds humans cannot hear but that elephants hear and understand. I do not doubt this. But I think, no, I do not simply think, this time I am certain, that when the image floats up, the elephant makes no sound. I am certain that if the phone rang, the elephant would not pick it up.

I meet the guy in a café on a side street. People in the life congregate here and so do the people who hunt them. My appointment is with a hunter, an agent. The agent has nothing to do with the boy in the negative and yet I sense he comes from the same roll of film. We meet in the parking lot out front and walk in together. The agent cuts through the dining room to a bar in the back and then heads for a corner table under a wall-mounted television that has just enough sound to mask conversation and yet never enough sound so that a person in the bar could actually follow the program flickering across the screen. The bar is all but empty, but still the agent takes the corner table and sits with his back to the wall. He puts a small black case on the table in front of him and I know this is the gun. Nothing is said about the matter. Nothing is said clearly at all. In fact the agent can barely risk a mutter and I must lean forward and study his lips as he speaks in order to have a prayer of understanding him.

I order a glass of wine, the agent makes do with a light beer he barely sips. His eyes never cease moving, and while he talks they sweep across the bar like security cameras in a bank. He is an unsmiling man, and he wants to be here and he does not want to be here. Everything is confidential and not to be repeated. Okay? Sure. But then what is the point of talking at all? I know this is all a ruse, a delicate ruse. The agent wants me to know something, but in his very bones he is upset by his need to talk. It is like a weakness he cannot control or even acknowledge, this desire for talking. When you live under a code of silence, talk is difficult, but eventually the silence becomes the real difficulty, the reality of never writing down what you do, of never seeing your actions on paper, of never repeating what you know to be true. No matter how hard an agent tries, this silence grows heavier and heavier, and in the end, agents always come to some bar and meet someone like me and say things not to be repeated that they know will be repeated. And this entire treason against self is caused by a need to maintain sanity, to break down the silence and finally speak, even if only in a mutter half buried by the noise of a television purring.

Three Mexican guys enter the bar wearing leather coats that fall below their waists, the kind of coats that easily cover guns tucked into waistbands, and I can see their entry in the movement of the agent's eyes and I do not need to turn to take them in, I can sense their presence from the slight movement of the agent's hand toward the small black case holding the gun, a movement barely perceptible and one that does not involve the rest of the agent's body, which is very erect in a chair, shoulders squared back, head almost robotically rigid, only the eyes softly scanning the room and the eyes are hard and have the look of a noose slowly tightening around a throat. Then the Mexicans sit down across the room and start chattering, order chips and beer, and do not look at the agent. I can tell all this without looking around, it is written clear as day on the absolutely blank face of the agent.

Slowly, the agent's muttering becomes understandable and for a while I listen as if it were late at night and some disc jockey was purring on as the car roars down the interstate and the voice on the radio is barely audible but still there, that sense of hearing not words but sounds that are clues to words and unconsciously translating those sounds into possible sentences. I knew it would get no better than this. I had met the agent once before and that time the muttering had been the same even though we were in the agent's office. No one can be trusted, and certainly no place, no phone, no piece of paper can ever be trusted. Nothing can be trusted, which is why talking is such a damn nuisance. That time in the office the agent had spoken for twenty minutes and not once during those twenty minutes did he directly look at me, not for a second.

The small black case rests on the hard wood near the agent's now relaxed hand. The mutter says, "Yeah, I'll tell you about that asshole, the fucker beat us, got his fucking charges dropped by some dickhead fed judge, and shit, we'd had him for months and he hadn't given us a fucking thing, he'd given up nothing, and so the fucking judge said he was free and then the border assholes moved in, right there in the courthouse, to take him into their custody 'cause they were going to deport his fucking ass, boom, just like that. And we were pissed, so were the other guys, because we knew he was fucking dirty and man he was big, he wasn't just some fucking punk, he was high up, and I'll tell you what happened. One little quick phone call over there to one of their uniforms and we gave them the time and the place and the bridge and that was it, case closed. Like the papers say, he was last seen getting into a car with what looked to be federal officers right after he crossed the bridge and goddamn his family hasn't heard from him, you know. Because everybody over there figured he must have talked, that only by talking could he have gotten sprung."

I am all ears because he knows about the walk over the bridge and the magical disappearance. It is an unsolved mystery on the televisions and in the newspapers. And here is the explanation swirling within this mutter of barely audible sound. It is a negative briefly floating into view, the face coming closer and closer and then suddenly sinking back into darkness.

I finally ask, "Where do you think he is?"

The agent smiles a kind of smirk and says, "You know better than to ask that."

I have tried to explain the room to myself, the fact that I find it everywhere and the drapes are closed and the light restricted to the tip of my cigarette and the glow of the clock. I have noticed how this glow is almost always red and wondered who decides this. I have seen them by the bedsides in homes glowing a blue-green, a few even a stark white, but not in the motels and never in the room. Once in a while the room comes without a clock and I am stricken when this happens even though I seldom care what time it is. Still, I feel insecure without the glowing clock, the face changing every minute, sometimes even flicking off the seconds like fleas jumping off a dog.

The room must be free of light, but sound never matters. I do not care about the roar of interstates, even if they rattle the windows through the night. I never complain about ten o'clock drunks horsing around in the pool. I can sit in bliss while a television blares in the room next door. My ears all but vanish once I enter the room. My eyes grow large in the blackness. My sense of touch is limited, a soft move of the hand to locate the ashtray in the dark, a flick of the wrist to knock off ash. The click to activate my lighter.

I grow calm. My heart slows. My breathing is very regular, a yogi's envy. My skin seems to sleep and the chill off the refrigeration unit never touches me.

I am dying and I know it. And I think I should be concerned about this transition. But the room soothes me and I cannot focus on my own death. And yet in the room, no matter where it is, I can feel my end come nearer. It seems to creep down some velvet lane toward me. I sometimes cannot get out of the chair. My limbs do not feel leaden or weak but something else. Vague, light, without substance. I think I should get a glass of water. Fifteen minutes, sometimes longer, will stream down the glowing clock face before I can make such a move.

I am not depressed. I think, This must be the approach of death. Acceptance.

Then the face will float in front of me, the face in the negative, and my mind will seem to move, and issues and questions will slowly come to me. My hands will flex, suddenly my fingers will curl back to my palm. Sometimes when the face draws nearer and seems to come into focus, my hand will form a fist. Once, I caught my fingers tapping on the tabletop. This surprised me since I normally do not tap my fingers. Or my foot.

I am sitting in the room. I have run all over the city, I have found the mother, I have talked to the reporter who saw the body or claims to have seen the body. I have had that drink with the agent. I have watched the woman in pigtails and her friends boost things from a gas station. I have never seen the Mexican's negative. But then the Mexican does not have the negative, never took the photograph. He would even tell me this if only I asked in the proper way, if I asked in a way that demonstrated I understood the situation.

I have the phone number in my billfold. Her number. If I take it out and then punch it out, a voice will answer. Then I will have a name, have one as soon as I say hello. Then she will have a name. And a face. A body. A past, present, and future. A scent, some kind of perfume, her own cut to her hair, her lipstick, her nail polish. She will have special lingerie, special colors, things she eats, and things she does not eat. Things she has not tried.

I will be roughly the same. A face, a past, addresses, bills, friends, business contacts. And a first name. Once it begins, it all floods in. I will walk on specific carpets across specific rooms, rooms with names, the bedroom, the kitchen, the living room, the rec room, the dining room, perhaps a parlor. There may be a piano. A south light, a north light. There will be potted plants and these plants will probably need food or water.

And she will laugh, laugh easily. Smile too.

I told you I might call.

Just fish out the number, punch it in. Hear the dial tone. We met once before. She will talk about that.

I can hear her voice, and then I sink back into myself and the voice fades away.

I should decide one way or another. I know the room is essential but I am using up the room. My habit is getting too large, the room is taking me over. I can feel it in the calm, the dying.

I reach for the phone on the table, then stop.

I think, I'll light another cigarette.

She will have plans, people we should meet. High school yearbooks, poems she has written. Hobbies, also. Maybe she knits or does stitchery. Paints, even. What kind of paintings?

I will put the call off. I am not quite ready.

A Mexican is at the wheel. The city huddles under a gray sky and a wind whips out of the west. Out the car window, people walk home from work, bent over in the wind, plastic bags of groceries swaying in their hands. Girls of thirteen and fourteen stream past wearing blue smocks, having finished ten- to twelve-hour shifts in the factory. They look like robots except for their faces, which are elaborately defined by makeup. Their hair tends to be long and the bangs are greased so they stand up. They all wear running shoes and seem barely five feet tall.

The city comes and goes. Bare ground appears and then suddenly a slum streams past, shacks made of plastic and salvaged boards and tarpaper lining the crooked streets. No one has water or electricity. Smoke fills the air now, and as dusk comes down, kerosene lamps come on here and there. A few stars dot the sky, hunting through the clouds, and suddenly a huge sweep of creosote takes over and the desert truly begins.

The Mexican pulls off the pavement and heads down a bumpy dirt track for a mile or so. Then he stops and kills the engine.

He says, "Here is where they leave them."

I start out wanting the negative because it violates official truth, shows official truth to be a lie. And within this refutation of the lie rests the rock-hard notion that truth exists just like a stratum in the earth, perhaps a stratum ancient and hoary, something from the age of dinosaurs, but still there, down there, temporarily buried and denied the light of day. This stratum will be excavated and the world made right. That is how I think it began, assuming there was some moment on the clock when the thing cleanly began. But somewhere in all those rooms I have come to realize, without ever thinking about it, that belief in this stratum of truth implies a tidy order, implies a restoration, the restoration of a kind of model community where the streets are clean, the lawns mowed, the curtains crisp, the children well-mannered, a village that looks alarmingly like some white clapboard village in New England. And I can't believe that, can't believe in the stratum itself, because the world I live in and taste and know is not rock. It is movement, some dark-night moves, some shouts in daylight at celebrations, but still movement.

The hard stratum of truth, this ground does not matter. Desire matters, but not simply wanting things. Wanting means a belief that all can be made right. And that is too much to hope for, that is not even something to hope for. The thing is movement and it is not something to be fixed or even repaired. It is not a sputtering engine in a car that can be fiddled with. Really fixing things means tinkering not only with the car but with the driver. It means first going to the room and enduring the room and tasting death coming nearer and nearer on velvet. And then leaving the room. Yes, I realize, it means also leaving the room.

I feel the cold metal and think of the hollow-tipped bullets sleeping in the chamber. I have unzipped the black nylon case, but the gun is still out of view as I reach in and stroke the smooth barrel, run my finger across the trigger guard. It's a Brazilian copy of a Smith & Wesson, a knockoff of some real thing I bought near a Ute reservation out of state. There was a waiting period, but the storeowner was ticked off at all the rules and regulations. I handed over cash and it was done. I remember the cool air outside the gun store, the breath coming off the Rockies with a promise of flowers in mountain meadows and women, naked, running careless through the lush tall grass.

Now it rests on the table in the dark.

I think it would be easy. One tug of the finger. I drink red wine and savor the thought. I know soon the face will float up from the negative and be in the room. But just now, a drink is in order. I have always considered the gun foolish and yet essential.

Not suicide. No, I want an ending and that is where the gun can help and why I carry it. I must simply fire it at some-one and then see what happens. The knowing will appear in the flash. Explode in front of my eyes. A brief action, then, well, then I do not care. I will have asserted my existence and their existence. Maybe I will go to that bar across the line, the one people disappear from and never again reappear. Sit there with the gun, wait. And then make things happen and be solid and firm and three-dimensional.

This happens more often than I like to admit, these mo-ments in the room with the gun when I dream of creating a world of order and acts and consequences with the gun. When I read things or watch movies, I notice how often the gun appears to solve something or move something along. I always resent these moments and see them as false, as evasions of the real highways along which life courses. I hate these moments because they insist on the existence of endings and these endings insist that things exist to move down a path toward a destiny. I know these solutions are lies. I cannot abide them.

Yet I keep the gun, just like the characters in the movies. I share this need that apparently is common in audiences. I want to evade, to run away and fire the gun and avoid the room. Yes, that's it, I think, avoid the room. That face floating. Bang! And it will all be gone. Maybe I can become some small item in a newspaper. There will be an investigation of sorts and it will conclude that nothing about motive can be determined. The autopsy will find me clean, not a trace, and so that will also be a dead end.

No one will claim the body, a cremation will follow, then the file will go into the drawer, perhaps a John Doe if I am thoughtful and ditch all my identification first. Prints? There must be prints somewhere but the system is not that good and, who knows, they may not even run them.

The wine is rich on my tongue, the gun cool to my touch. I rub my finger over the tooth of the sight on the end of the barrel, a hash mark of metal that in theory impales a person in the line of sight, fastens on him and locks his fate into the trajectory of a bullet. The hollow-point will expand on contact and tear the hell out of him. That is its function.

Days and days go by, and I myself forget about it. But then it comes back, just like the face that floats, comes back and is suddenly solid, cool, and alarmingly large. An elephant in the room with me.

The gun is useless. I know that. But I cannot seem to give it up. The gun goes from room to room.

It is said to be near Yemen, somewhere out in the emptiness of the Saudi Arabian desert. No one has ever been there and returned. They have tried, there are stories about these efforts. But no real reports. This is the elephant graveyard, the place the beasts lumber toward when they feel death on their wrinkled hides. There are also stories of people following dying elephants in order to find the graveyard. In these accounts, the elephants always go in circles and befuddle their pursuers.

There are rumors that the graveyard is the seat of magic chants, powerful knowledge that could bring peace to the world, or destruction. Guardians are said to keep watch over the graveyard and to kill any visitors. It is unclear just how this fact came to be known, since no visitor could report it. And there is the problem of crossing from Africa to the Arabian Peninsula. I do not even want to think of the journey from, say, Asia or the Bronx Zoo.

But I believe deeply in the graveyard and in knowing the tales that the graveyard implies. The knowing that cannot be escaped, not after one knows. And yet cannot be articulated. The price of living, I think.

Some of the stories say that the elephants, presumably spewing forth from the graveyard, will lead humans to the new land, the promised land. This part I doubt. I think these stories come from people who have not been to the room or even heard rumors of the room.

The key thing, for me, is the dying, the sense of dying, the movement to the desert. The guardians of course are important, but it is the going to the place, the sense of knowing. And the silence about the matter.

Back in the room, I begin to recover and I can feel this recovery as the velvet footsteps approach and sensation leaves me. The refrigeration is on high but I do not feel cold. Or hot. The clock glows and becomes almost blinding. The fabric of my shirt rubs me raw and weighs tons. I am imprisoned by my clothes.

I run through some options for a few moments. I savor the indignation of a child who has discovered that the adult world is a fraud. I move on to the indignation of an investigator who believes in the world but discovers there is one area where deception is being practiced and must be exposed so that the world can be cleansed and made whole again. I consider the stance of a politician who can listen to the revelations and say *Yes, but*—and then shrug, the politician who knows it is not a perfect world and that some things can never be changed. I am the philosopher questioning the existence of everything, even the existence of the sentence questioning the existence of everything. I am the voice saying things are relative. I am the critic saying yes, but photographs lie and at the very best are simply statements of blindness by an individual or a culture or both. I can be a storyteller but still destroy my story by explaining that it is all simply a deception played out through point of view.

Or I can go to the room and wait.

What I can no longer do is imagine. I used to be up to that.

A negative requires light eating at film and then processing. The print hangs on a line drying, a face gleaming on the shiny surface.

Tina died on July 21 and Sissy and Winkie grieved, stayed for three days at the grave, and left a favored toy, an old tire, atop Tina's burial mound. Joanna also died on July 21, two years after Tina's passing. Joanna perished when Winkie, a 7,600-pound Asian elephant, crushed her. Joanna was a thirty-six-year-old petite woman who spent eight years tending to the elephants at a sanctuary for damaged beasts in Tennessee.

Winkie was born in Burma in 1966 and caught in the wild

and peddled to a greater world. She wound up in Madison, Wisconsin, where she replaced Winkie One, a rather angry elephant who had murdered a four-year-old girl visiting the zoo. Winkie Two had anger also and attacked several keepers—which is how she got her ticket punched to the elephant sanctuary in Tennessee. There she became the great friend of Sissy and, it was thought, of Joanna.

Then Winkie killed Joanna and no one knows why.

There is a line between us and them that we must not cross, or if we do cross it, we must accept our peril. They are other nations and these nations must be accepted and approached with caution.

But there is an even greater risk: not crossing that line. Staying safe, never reaching out for the negative of the dead boy. She looks so frail in the photograph standing next to an elephant against the maze of the Tennessee forest. When I was a boy I dreamed of riding a snake about the countryside, sat envious by the creek as the carp leaped from the green water and then returned to the depths denied me.

We know that elephants mourn their dead and increasingly we admit this fact. They have been known to cover elephant bones found in the forest. There is the matter of Sissy and Winkie placing that tire on Tina's grave. They have been seen standing in a circle with shoulders touching after the death of a herd member. We have made notes on this matter. But then, I have a friend who observed a wake held by a bunch of ravens over a fallen comrade. When I was a boy, there was that dog that went down to the basement and starved to death after its master died. I was three or four then and the old man would whittle little dogs from wood and give them to me.

It is not clear how the elephants under Joanna's care feel about her murder. Or what they think of Winkie for killing the woman who tended to their hungers and hurts. It is not clear what we think of the curse on that Madison zoo where

Annie died of a foot infection and was replaced by Winkie One who slaughtered a child who was replaced by Winkie Two who has now committed homicide. They are very intelligent, they have the fabled memory, they need the companionship of other elephants, they are large and seldom use their size against us.

A Mexican dictator once noted that nothing ever happens in Mexico. Until it happens.

We want them to like us, we want this very much. We want them to forgive us, since we know elephants only by being part of a kidnapping ring.

I am part of a species where many find it forbidden to cross religious lines. Or race lines. I want to cross bloodlines. I want to risk my life for another organism, I want to shed my culture and join another culture, to meld with the beasts, to destroy the notion of parks and zoos and reserves and flow in a river of blood off some Niagara and be pounded into another life in the red pool below, the pool that churns and roars with spray and licks one's being with an overwhelming undertow.

I will leave the room, follow the trumpeting of the elephants, and want not.

The problem is the unacceptable answer. Find the negative, feel the death, and yet the deaths keep coming because people need to live and the killing ensures that others live and prosper. But still, finding the negative is an act. Going to the elephant ground where the maimed souls of zoos and circuses are healed by human kindness, well, that is an act even if it results in your own death. Joanna in one photo is stroking the trunk of an elephant. Her eyes are closed and so are those of the elephant. Her skin looks smooth, the hide of the elephant looks eroded by life.

When Winkie lived at the Madison zoo, she spent most of her years chained in a pen or cell or cage—what do we call it?—with a cement floor. Like a lot of captive elephants she had foot troubles from the hard surfaces we always seem to provide. Some of her attacks were on humans tending her ailing feet.

Then Freedom Day came and she was led to a big tractor-trailer and wooed with a dozen watermelons. After that, it was the long ride to Tennessee. All the press accounts on Winkie note that she had a bad reputation.

Just when is an elephant guilty? In India, an elephant was slated for death because it had killed at least twenty people in a five-month murder spree outside a city where steel was made. Its m.o. was trampling humans. But trackers concluded that at least eighteen elephants fitted the description of the killer. The villages in question made illegal booze and the elephants were attracted by the aroma coming off the stills, would commandeer the hooch, get loaded and then trample anyone who tried to stop their binges. In another region of India, wild herds of elephants were plundering an army base. They'd take out the electric fence by dropping trees on the lines. They'd put out fires created by the soldiers to keep the elephants at bay by hosing them down. Once inside, the elephants would grab rum bottles, crack them open on a hard surface and guzzle. They also took flour and sugar. Then they'd vanish back into the jungle.

In the medieval bestiaries, elephants eat mandrake so that the male can overcome his reluctance to copulate. Then the pair travels to a place near Paradise, and the female gives birth and wades into the Pool of Guilt. The male stands guard and protects her from any dragon that might approach. Other details gleaned by ancestors: elephants fear mice, politely give greetings to any people they encounter, and serpents flee the smoke rising off their burning hides or bones.

In the ancient world, Pliny the Elder realized that elephants come closest to human intelligence, exhibit wisdom, give due respect to religion, are gentle and harmless unless provoked. He also noted that the mere breath of an elephant would drive serpents from their holes.

We are always on the outside and we cannot really look in. Winkie is believed by some to be in deep remorse. There are observations of elephants weeping, of tears rolling down their cheeks, but this fact does not tell us what is going on in their minds.

I think the snake sleeping by my foot recognizes me and finds me innocent and safe. I think the cardinal on the nest is calm when I am near because of my fine nature. But I can never know.

I think the negative of the body of the dead boy will bring me closer to truth and that I will leave the room and move in the world and by that fact I will change the world.

I will become like Winkie, a creature of bad reputation who strikes out.

I hear footsteps in the hall, the sound of a key in a lock, a door opening and then closing. Someone is safe for the night.

Winkie's eye is swollen. They think maybe fire ants bit her. She has come in for water, and one keeper examines her eye but does not touch the swelling. Joanna hands Winkie the hose. The elephant seems very calm. The woman moves to the elephant's right side to have a closer look at the eye. Winkie spins, knocks her across her chest and face, then steps on her. They bury her on the grounds of the sanctuary. The staff concludes the death was an accident. Winkie will not be killed. They believe she is suffering from post-traumatic stress disorder.

I think I know better than to complain about things. I feel only one thing. I feel tears seeping from my eyes and falling down my face. I do not make a sound. I do not feel foolish about the weeping. I feel calm. My breathing is regular.

———

I think it is all about rhythm, about a distant beat, and if one catches that beat and keeps it in one's mind and in one's cells, lives it in the very protoplasm, softly swings to it like the Mexican, then, well, one can get by, get through. The beat is irregular and at times almost inaudible, it can sometimes reach a point where minutes pass between the strokes on the drumhead, but it goes on and on and strings things together, splashes colors, draws faces, floods the air with scent, moves the sky overhead, and explodes in fiery storms on the skin of the sun. All lingerie is dependent on hearing this beat, the holy writings also, and kites playing in the March skies. I think the room is killing me because it is killing the beat, smothering the beat. I can, I think at times, hear the scream of the skin on the drumhead as it is punctured and all the life goes out of it. I know what I am thinking is nonsense, something I lack the guts to say out loud, this belief in the importance of the beat. A conceit, a gloss, a spin on the pain. A sly trick of the mind. Perhaps what I am thinking is something worse, something much worse. Perhaps this notion of the importance of the beat is clever. And clever is a knife in the guts of life itself. When the negative comes into view in the dark, the face floating, the beat slowly recedes and the strokes grow further apart. For a long time, I thought this was good, a sign of clarity. A sign that I was nearing a truth. I thought killing noise brought me closer to the core of whatever is life.

I thought the room was the cure.

I think of the elephant. The huge animal stands by the roadside in a state far to the south. He belongs to a circus but they cannot afford to feed him. So each day, his keeper takes him to the major highway and leaves him to browse along its shoulders. An elephant must eat some massive amount of plants, surely some number that reaches tons, in order to stay alive. The cars go by, people stare, the elephant feeds.

I think of the intelligence of elephants and that something must run through their minds. Their memory is famous and some think they have a sense of music. Also, they live many, many years and this memory is chock-full of experiences. Once, I flipped on a television, I cannot remember where or when, it was one of those nature programs and a bunch of elephants had returned, after some weeks, to where their former leader had fallen and died. They circled the corpse and silently stood there, a seeming memorial. Then after a while they plodded back into the brush and took their thoughts with them.

I cling to these memories because whatever I mean by knowing, I sense they share. And yet they do not go to the room, they stand by a highway and feed. They plod on into the brush. They recognize death but still seem not to falter. They do not need the darkness that is essential to me in the room.

Velvet, a movement in the room that has the feel of velvet, so soft the sound. I realize I am dying. I am neither hot nor cold. The beat grows yet more infrequent, the spaces between the downstrokes almost eras, epochs, eons, long spaces between the beats.

I must recover my name and my face. That at least. My hair color, my height, the tint in my eyes. A voice with inflections, a voice made somewhere, a voice with a place and roots in something. A past, a present, a future. All the tenses.

I reach for the phone.

But I stop.

I feel I am dying in the room. But I put off the phone. I sense that the phone and the phone call and the names and faces might kill me.

I will smoke a cigarette first. Yes, that is what I will do.

I will think about the phone.

Ocean

There was a time.

Everything blurred.

And this felt right. I wake up by the river amid the salt cedar and smell the brown water purling past on its way to the Gulf. The stars are still, the moon down, and I light the stove under coffee. I got here after midnight and do not remember eating.

I drive for days and days and then descend for a night, a week, a month. The women are scattered about the ground, always ahead of me or behind me.

I carry a bag, a machete, a pad, the stove, a notebook. The words drive me, not the truck, and in some way I did not understand then, or understand now, I am chasing the words. Not a sentence or a vocabulary but a strand of words that would freeze the blur into a clear frame—black and white with a grainy surface and no gloss. I should have paid more attention to the women.

I'll get up from the clean sheets, go to the kitchen and make coffee and she will rise and come out and I'll kiss her and smell the nape of her neck and run my hand on the curve of her ass and we will not say a word as our hips grind into each other. The early light will filter through the windows. I will bend down, move her robe apart, and lick her nipple, and in my mind I am already moving down the road.

We have coffee and the desert sun bakes outside the window. The bed is made. I am packed. I rub my fingers on her blouse and feel her nipple harden. I reach underneath and my hand flows under her bra and I caress her breast and she does not smile, her full lips tighten, her eyes focus tightly. She knows I have already left. I take her hand, lead her into the bedroom, undo the belt on her jeans and slowly wriggle them over her generous hips and to the floor. She falls back on the bed, my face is buried between her legs, then I mount her and she falls into a rhythm and birds sing outside and the house is so tidy as the bed slams against the wall and violates the order of the cups in the cabinets, that tiny stash of marijuana she keeps in the freezer, the carefully dusted bric-a-brac on the shelves, and now her face relaxes as an orgasm shudders through her body and I hold her arms down as she desires.

Outside, the truck loaded, the engine running, she stares at me and begins to weep.

"What's wrong?"

"Get the fuck out of here. I don't want you watching me cry."

At the end of the dirt lane, I pause and wonder whether I should visit the sex therapist, the woman who clerks, or the woman in Mexico. I am not a wanderer, I just wander. Wherever I call home I flee from at least two hundred days a year.

She buzzes me up to her apartment in New York. I can see a water tower on the roof across the street as I hold her in my arms. She opens my fly, I stroke her body. She falls backward and the coffee table crashes. Then she instantly gets up and we go to the room and cool air flows in from the open window.

When I leave in a few days she is astounded that I have consumed an entire jar of instant coffee.

Outside the hotel window is a fake beach and lagoon. She leans across the chair and stares out as I fuck her. We stay two days and hardly speak. I've come to this city because of her birthday.

I cross the line and vanish into Sonora. For days, I sit on the patio and stare at the banana tree and the coffee tree. I hear parrots in the growth. She comes out of the kitchen. When I arrived she sprawled on the bed naked and I let fifteen one-hundred-dollar bills flutter down on her body.

Now she says, "I feel like a wife," and she means this as a mark of contempt.

I am silent.

On the mountain the forest is disappearing. I invent a project to save it and she plunges into this work. I drink bad wine and black coffee. I come and go on jobs. In ten days, I raise ten thousand dollars for the project. My own income disappears into the cause. I walk the forest. I stare at the fresh stumps. I decide that I want to live for twenty-five more years, and at the end of that sentence I will return here and buy a case of cold beer and sit under a blooming amapa tree and drink it all, comforted by the knowledge that the tree has survived only because of my actions.

The cruise control is set at eighty-five as we cross the Mojave in the night.

"The cops," he explains, "won't pull you over at night out here."

I look into the blackness and can smell the fear that washes over the cops. This is the ground of drunks, of the broken, of drifters, of the hitchhiker with murder in his eyes. Even during the blaze of day this is still the country of the night, this strand of interstate with people fleeing someplace and dreaming some other place. I pitch an empty beer can.

"They're afraid," he continues, "afraid of all the goddamn nuts out on the road."

We have three guns, pistols. Beer, but I am the only one drinking. The trick, he tells me, is to toss the cans. Some guys, he notes, pitch them artfully out the window and into the air-stream of the truck so that they clatter and collect in the bed of the pickup. Cop pulls you over and sees all those empty beer cans and what in the hell can he conclude?

He is a man of technique, little rules and procedures for everything. He is plagued by migraines and these regulations.

We carry a set of mauls of various weights. And a keg of spikes. Drive the big nails into the living wood, post a sign on the grove warning of this act. Then it is too risky for timbering, liable to shatter a saw in the mill, maybe kill someone.

All this makes a certain sense to me. I am not depressed, I simply know I am on the losing side, that the trees go, the mountains go, the desert goes, the rivers go, the wildlife goes. An obituary of a friend read that he was born a hundred years too late and died a hundred years too early. I knew what that meant and that I was trapped within that same time frame and faced the same reality. All of my days and nights would be caught up in this war I was losing, and nothing I wrote or anyone else wrote would stop it.

Daniel Shays faced this kind of time. So did the stout men of the Whiskey Rebellion. So did the Molly Maguires, assuming the Mollies actually existed. No one gets to pick their time. You only get to decide how you spend that time.

The federal trial of a friend is in a small town. The room is a pale blue-green, the benches worn wood. The witness wears a brown suit, white shirt, tie. He is the government infiltrator. His voice is soft and vanishes in the space of the courtroom. He tells of when he got the money.

"You met with him alone in a pickup truck?"

"Yes."

I think the money is my own, that thousand or fifteen hundred I dropped off in a brown grocery bag. But I do not know this for certain and I never ask.

"You knew him to be a spiritual man?"

"I think that's questionable."

During recess, I talk to my friend in the corridor.

"I want to be a bargain-basement writer," he says, "write second-rate novels and books about nature, not spend two and a half years like this."

But he got caught and now he is inside the belly of the whale and he cannot escape at will.

Outside the courthouse I meet a woman. She says she and her husband have a vacant rental where I can spend the night. The room smells antiseptic, the linoleum gleams. The bed is narrow.

Later that night I hear a knock. She leaves in the morning.

I am high in the mountains wandering a grove of aspen and counting the winter kill of elk. The sky is blue and finally I can smell the earth. I look down into the meadow by the river and see two cow elk jump a rail fence. The brown of their bodies shimmers. The grass waves in a light breeze.

At night I sit on the porch of a log cabin in the cold and drink wine. When I turn in, she is under the covers, her black hair smelling fresh, her lips red and full. I see the moon rise through the window.

There have been many hard times when no one had hope. Sometimes this knowledge helps and sometimes it does not. Verdun stank with gore for less than a year. The official tally runs 337,231 French, 337,000 German.

A French soldier, Alfred Joubaire, scribbles a note in his diary, "They must be crazy to do what they are doing now.... I cannot find words to express my feelings.... People are insane!" All this murder in less than ten square kilometers, a little over six square miles, the German crown prince watching, a huge mortar tossing death and called sweetly Big Bertha. Louis Barthas makes a note: "In front of us on the floor the two I had witnessed ablaze, lay rattling. They were so unrecognizably mutilated that we could not decide on their identities. One of them died that same night. In a fit of insanity the other hummed a tune from his childhood, talked to his wife and his mother, and spoke of his village."

I have my own numbers of slaughter. There are fifteen hundred ships putting two million miles of net a year—thirty-five thousand miles a night. Everything dies. The whales also. The ocean called Pacific, in the northern waters. These numbers mean nothing to me because I can imagine neither the ocean nor the deaths.

I live a blur, that is what I remember of those times, the sense of a blur.

That and my decision to go to sea.

The father failed at everything he tried. Then his sons went forth and began to fail. At age twenty, Herman ships out as a cabin boy and sees Liverpool in England. A year later, he bums his way west through Buffalo, the Great Lakes, down the Mississippi, then back up the Ohio. He can find no work but he is little suited to work. He cannot spell well, his penmanship is poor, his schooling hit-and-miss. He goes to New Bedford and sails on a whaler for a voyage of at least two years. Whalers get low pay and are seldom in port. Their wives call their dildos "He's-at-home."

Years later he wrote about how men on docks stare at ships and men on ships in port stare at shore. He thought "of week days pent up in lath and plaster—tied to counters, nailed to benches, clinched to desks. How then is this? Are the green fields gone? What do they here?"

So I go to sea.

That was long ago and just yesterday. For years I turned the voyage over in my mind, then buried it and walked away from its grave. But it lingers still. I could never write a real account. The ship sailed forth to save the seas from murder at the hands of men. The ship sailed forth wrapped in the glow of green thoughts and vegetarian meals and peace on earth.

I cannot remember how I got to port in the far northwest. A plane, I assume. I was living in Mexico, the forest was being cut down, death was in the air, and I left for blue water and for some kind of answer. At the time, I told myself I wanted to take part in striking back at something. I wanted a physical act to replace meetings and words and speeches and strange acts of personal thrift and virtue.

I wanted to say yes, shout yes, be yes. I wanted to accept but not submit.

I took pills for seasickness. And I took Herman Melville's *Moby-Dick*.

In this time of blurring, I would visit this woman. She had qualities I envied. Nothing coarsened her, nothing. Not violence, not crime, not punishment. She remained pure, always. We would shower together and I always had the same thought: You will never need soap and I will never find anything to cleanse me.

I would rise in the night at two or three A.M. and tell her I was leaving, that I was going to work. This was always true. I'm obsessed with rising before the sun and being at my labors. I have a folk belief that this simple act will keep me on the straight and narrow path.

She would bolt upright, accuse me of some variation of infidelity, grab my cock and suck it lest I venture into the dark hours without being drained. She saw other women in my eyes.

I loved her for those moments.

Once, she told me, "I just want things to be nice. You know?"

Yes, I know. I want spring, the water flowing in the milk house cooling the squeezings from the udders, the March winds blowing clothes on the line, fish jumping in the creek, linen fresh, chicken frying in the blackened pan, smiles on the women, calm in the men, corn cracking in the July heat, dogs panting.

But I must go down to the sea again, that big water we hide behind a lying phrase where we say a storm went safely out to sea.

In the lobby bar a piano plays soft and forgettable tunes. Wine, yes, wine, her eyes are bright and anxious. She insists on ordering, has accepted a kind of philosophy of life where you order everything, you make a pyramid of things in rank of significance and then act on this list, and when you are done, well, you tell others proudly that you get it.

She prides herself on her mind and on her body.

Once, she stood before me naked and said, "Look, I'm thirty with the body of a fourteen-year-old," and gave off a girlish giggle.

Once, we were sitting on a couch in her fine home and she got on the floor and said, "Come in my mouth."

Once, I wrote a book about a mountain in order to encourage other human beings to cease laying rough hands on it. I heard a knock at the door and she was there and she said, "Why did you write this?"

She believes in software, and at the time, I believed in mountains.

She raises the wineglass, a fine white, and delicately sips.

The other tables are crowded, the hotel is full, people come here for vacations and so become people of a resort. The lobby bar looks out through a glass wall at the lush grounds and inviting blue pool.

Suddenly she is standing.

I rise.

She takes my hand and we leave the bar, cross the busy lobby weaving through a throng of people. Some convention is going on, everyone wears a nametag.

She opens a metal door and we enter the stairwell. She leads me up floor after floor.

Finally she stops and drops my hand.

She reaches under her dress and pulls off her panties.

I say nothing.

Then she lies on the floor and looks up at me.

When we reenter the lobby, her panties are in her purse.

We return to the small table, the piano, the glasses of wine.

She smiles and glances down and stares through the glass tabletop.

My cum is dribbling down her leg.

Sometimes I think of her when I struggle to create order, to make lists, to ask questions and provide answers.

So I went down to sea. I was looking for my death and I was saying yes. I suspect you think it was about women or drink or drugs or stories men tell each other.

But it was about ocean. And, yes.

The swells pound in the cold night, the air sags, a mist dabbed with snow, but we do not care as we stand on deck and drink Scotch from coffee mugs. The radar has gone blank, the green blips streaking away into the big empty of the pond. Chicken Bob is happy now, his eyes glow, his frame jumps with energy. He is on a roll and there is nothing in the nothing of the North Pacific that can compete with the torrent of words spewing from his mouth.

"I'd say on a scale often it's a ten!" he shouts. "We rammed two of the son of a bitches. I'm forty-eight years old and I've finally gotten some good ram."

Bob's been around. In the fog banks that blur everyone's past, he was one of the founders of the big organization devoted to peace and to things green back when it was a clutch of Canadian lefties and potheads, back when it put its bodies between whales and Soviet harpoons, back when Chicken Bob made the main decisions by throwing the I Ching. Back when it was an original idea. Then it became successful, then it fell apart for him. So Bob took a walk, bought a chicken farm, and became Chicken Bob. He wrote the books, scribbled magazine pieces, trotted the world, made it as the environmental reporter on television. This hasn't been enough. Now he's out on the deck with that hoard of Scotch as the ship plows through the sea twelve hundred miles off the West Coast. The bow has holes you could pitch a dog through—ah, those rammings. No matter. The ship is still electric. A ten.

Aquagirl comes out on deck. She's covered with grime from the greasy, rusty tub, but that figures, she's a real worker. I have watched her since the moment I came onboard. She is strong, silent, self-contained. Chicken Bob when he first laid eyes on her said, "Ah, a biker broad." I had not expected to meet somebody like her on this kind of voyage. She grabs me by the arm and says, "Let's go to my room, I've got a half gallon of rum." Chicken Bob's eyes light up. He's a warrior of the rainbow and it takes fuel to keep the colors coming.

He went mainly because he'd failed at everything on land. He took a whaler out of Massachusetts and then deserted ship for one of those lovely islands in the South Pacific where he'd heard the women will do anything you wish and the men, well, the men eat other men, eat sailors such as himself. He works in a field, he wanders beaches, he joins another ship, sails, he deserts again. He is put in chains, he is released. He winds up in Hawaii and joins the U.S. Navy. After four years at sea, he returns to the United States.

Herman Melville is now grounded. And out of his skull books explode for seven years.

One spring I sat down at a restaurant in the desert with friends. Down at the end of the table sat a guy I did not know, the Captain. He noted that he'd had bad luck with reporters because they tended not to show up for voyages when the time finally arrived to head out into the ocean blue. I said, "Okay, I'll go." Then I asked, "What exactly is the mission?" I was going because I was tired of listening. I was so tired of listening that I was flooded with a murderous kind of energy, a desire to reach out with my hands and grab a throat and choke. Tired of listening to announcements of the end of nature, of new ruptures in the ozone, of some damnable greenhouse effect, of cancer lurking in everything I liked to eat. I was tired of television specials about dead elephants, of magazines shouting pollution as they dropped into my mailbox, tired of listening to friends bemoan the demise of planet earth. I was tired of listening. So I bought a bottle of Dramamine and walked onboard.

At that instant, there were thirty thousand miles of drift nets, each twenty to thirty miles long, floating out in the North Pacific every night, killing whales, dolphins, seals, tuna, salmon, steelheads, seabirds. There were a thousand ships, maybe fifteen hundred ships, flying the flags of Japan, Taiwan, and South Korea.

Melville in *Moby-Dick* asks "why all the living so strive to hush all the dead."

Everyone tosses out numbers of the dead.

Dall's porpoise, 20,000 to 30,000.

Northern fur seal, 50,000.

Seabirds, 1,000,000.

All this collateral damage so the drift-net fleet can catch something called the neon flying squid.

I do not know the scent of these creatures. They are names, like the capitals of nations I have never visited.

I cannot describe these creatures, I am ignorant of the pleasures of their flesh, they are words in a list, their vast dying silent and distant.

The beads click on my rosary and their destruction remains as distant and faint as the nailing of Jesus Christ to his cross one Friday afternoon.

The object is *Ommastrephes bartrami*. They come north for summer and feed on the boundary waters, that line where the warmer Pacific waters collide with the chill of the Arctic. One female can produce from 350,000 to 3.6 million eggs. An adult might hit eight pounds. The life span is about a year.

The ships send out those endless nets and dream of tons of squid. One study found the dream plays out this way: for a catch of 3,119,061 neon flying squid, a few other creatures died—914 dolphins, 22 marine turtles, 9,173 seabirds, and about 1,580,068 fish, fish called in the trade "nontargeted."

My eyes glaze.

The study found this neon-squid-fishing operation to be wasteful and destructive.

I go, and I go ignorant of the sea and its creatures. I would not know a neon squid if one slapped me in the face.

Ralph Waldo Emerson wrote in his essay "Nature" that "the instincts of the ant are very unimportant, considered as the ant's; but the moment a ray of relation is seen to extend from it to man, and the little drudge is seen to be a monitor, a little body with a mighty heart, then all its habits, even that said to be recently observed, that it never sleeps, become sublime."

I have always loathed this idea of nature as some symbol board that matters because it edifies human beings. And now I go to sea because of a neon squid I cannot even visualize and I expect this squid to somehow restore a semblance of meaning to my life. I must apologize to Emerson when I run into him.

Everything begins in innocence, we insist on this fact. Someone or some group in Japan develops a nylon monofilament net so strong, and yet all but invisible, that it becomes the best tool ever designed for deep-sea drift netting and this tool takes squid in numbers never dreamed of before and within three years the death is so vast the fleet is forced by the government to go far out to sea, and the albacore begin to vanish from the South Pacific and the Indian Ocean is plundered and there is an outcry and the fleet keeps growing and growing, shows up in the North Pacific, and no one can tally the results, except to say that this is the largest slaughter of living things since the time of the gray dying that science thinks may have been caused by some meteor strike. But this is not from outer space, this time the death comes from our inventive hands and zeal for food.

Within thirteen years of the weaving of these fine new nets, there is an industry of estimates and a torrent of numbers to describe what is happening in the North Pacific as the nets hunt the squid and accidentally take a million and a half albacore and a million and a half blue sharks and legions of other living things. One outlaw fleet in the Indian Ocean eventually is killing fifty sperm whales a year by accident, collateral damage the common coin of life now.

As I sleep or rise or eat or drink or dream or laugh, the nets rake the waters, nets that if laced together would girdle the earth.

As I live with a rattlesnake or lie in the room with the clock glowing and the glow of the cigarette between my fingers and that negative floating just behind my reach, the nets float on the deep with buoys and lights, float like necklaces across the deep water and take everything, take so much living tissue that sober men of clean habits think they might kill the seas or will kill the only form of the seas we can contemplate without horror, and still they roll, far from sight of land, lonely ships in big fleets spinning endless miles of nets into the wet commons of our kind, the oceans deep.

I never gave the nets and the catch that eventually lands on my plate a single thought before I went to sea.

In *Moby-Dick*, Melville wrote, "Evil is unspectacular and always human, and shares our bed and eats at our own table."

The neon squid are suspected at times of cannibalism.

Chicken Bob is trying to explain something to me. He drops acid, goes to the opera for a performance of *Carmen*. At intermission he stands in the clogged lobby when a friend walks past and says, "I just want to warn you—watch out for the woman in the blue dress."

He turns around and there is this fine-looking woman in a blue dress with little straps. She has no arms. They make eye contact and he becomes a man in bondage. Everyone else in the lobby is pretending that the woman with no arms does not exist.

Chicken Bob and the woman begin to talk. He is swimming in a sea of acid, the woman is determined not to cut loose the only person who has recognized her existence. He begins to feel good about himself, about admitting the armless woman to human fellowship. But he cannot break it off. Maybe it is the acid, but maybe it is something else.

I once read of a kind of amoebae that live under leaves, scattered dots in the forest. Then they come together in a lump, and this lump refashions itself into what looks to our eyes like an opium poppy. After a while—I've never gotten the timing down—the amoebae disperse, the flower gone, the meaning of the sudden union lost to our understanding.

Chicken Bob tells this to me and Aquagirl as she drinks rum from a mug on the deck on a cold sea teeming with neon squid.

The ship runs to about 600 tons and 297 feet. She once fished the North Atlantic, double hulled against the anger of those waters. Around the deck runs a band of concertina wire, above flies a black flag with skull and crossed monkey wrenches. The crew runs to twenty-three, average age thirty-one. Seven have been out on the waters before.

Kill flags for ships sunk—three Japanese, two Icelandic, two Spanish—are lined up on the side of the bridge.

Aboard, I meet warm faces and appraising eyes. Aquagirl's skin is smooth, eyes blue, a childlike grin, and a flat voice. She casts a cool eye on me and I can see I am found wanting. I go down to my assigned quarters below the water line. I toss my paperback of *Moby-Dick* on the lower bunk. I can hear the sigh of water softly brushing the hull in the calm of the harbor.

The ship must leave soon. There is another war in the Middle East, and the Captain fears a rise in fuel. The ship needs thirty thousand gallons for the voyage, burns twenty gallons of oil an hour. Topside, Aquagirl is back at work, no time to waste. On deck they're battening things down for the big water. There's a twenty-foot powerboat, a Zodiac, and a couple of rafts, that's it for the lifesaving gear. Life preservers hardly matter in the cold waters off the Aleutians or in the Siberian waters where Russian whalers practice their secret slaughter.

I watch the sun bounce off Aquagirl's golden hair as she bends to her task.

She ignores me.

I imagine her scent.

I am afraid of the deep.

He thought it would be quick and easy. Instead he's riding failure, three books in a row have failed to find an audience. He's married, got a child, and frantically scribbles for money.

After beginning *Moby-Dick,* Melville retreats from New York City and takes a farm in the Berkshires. He bonds with Nathaniel Hawthorne and with something called *nature.* He is thirty-one years old and he writes a friend in the city, "You should see the young perennial pines—the red blazings of the one contrasting with the painted green of the others, and the wide flushings of the autumn air harmonizing both. I tell you that sunrises & sunsets grow side by side in these woods, & momentarily moult in the falling leaves."

And then something shifts and the book begins to devour Melville. He erases all the safe places and suddenly he is writing about a crazy captain and a big whale. "All men live enveloped in whale-lines. All are born with halters round their necks; but it is only when caught in the swift, sudden turn of death, that mortals realize the silent, subtle, everpresent perils of life. And if you be a philosopher, though seated in the whaleboat, you would not at heart feel one whit more terror, than though seated before your evening fire with a poker, and not a harpoon, by your side."

Though Melville served for a time on a whaler, there is no evidence that he ever hefted a harpoon. Or learned much about whales during his stint on the ship. But then, the early books fabricated a sexual frolic in the South Pacific that seems far more fantasy than flesh.

John Steinbeck explained to a friend who visited as he slaved away on *The Grapes of Wrath* how he was simply a kind of serf to a book that was writing itself. Steinbeck had never been to Oklahoma. When he finished the book and it became a hit, he chartered a boat and fled to the deep water.

The ship was launched in 1963 to take cod from the waters between Iceland and Great Britain. After years of fishing it began its slide toward the scrapyard. This voyage, this campaign, was a detour.

The crew has no real purpose either, beyond this voyage. They come to the ship to fill blank spaces in wayward lives. One is recovering from a bad car wreck and heard about the voyage three weeks ago. He thought it sounded, well, interesting. Another guy says he is killing time while his own ship is in dry dock. "To go to sea—that's it, you leave your problems back on the pier."

The cook has been on the road since he was sixteen. He hopes the ship will put in at Honolulu because he figures he can flimflam a way from there to Bali and on Bali they have the best theater in the world, he's heard, stuff that will expand your mind. After that, he thinks he'll go to India. He doesn't really know who he is, he allows, but he says he loves finding out.

In the galley is a small notice: DON'T BE HAPPY, WORRY.

The Captain, who has no captain papers and like the crew and the ship is simply an invention, is anxious now to clear port. He is chunky, a tumble of salt-and-pepper hair, wears a large ring of Poseidon. His voice is low, eyes always alert and questioning. He smiles but seems incapable of relaxing. He plots now how to destroy drift nets. He thinks that about a ton of old scrap iron will take such a net to the bottom. At depth, its buoyancy pods will collapse. He also dreams of salvaging one such net, taking it to Washington, and hanging it on the Mall so people can see the magnitude of this killing device.

The Captain bristles easily and spouts statements like, "I don't believe in animal rights. What right do we have to give animals rights?"

He entertains few questions. All the answers arrived in his life a long time ago. He admits he has no idea how the engine on a ship works.

Chicken Bob and his cameraman share my quarters. The air is stale, the swish of the sea against the hull the only sense of life down below.

Chicken Bob spends his nights reading a pile of Conan the Barbarian comic books. He believes that this is a time of mass media and truth can only seep through on the fringes of this culture.

I sprawl on the bunk and read under a faint overhead light about Jack London's savage man, Wolf Larsen. The voice on the page says, "Could we but find time and opportunity and utilize the last bit and every bit of the unborn life that is in us, we could become the fathers of nations and populate continents. Life? Bah! It has no value. Of cheap things it is the cheapest. Everywhere it goes begging. Nature spills it out with a lavish hand. Where there is room for one life, she sows a thousand lives, and it's life eats life till the strongest and most piggish life is left."

Down the hall is the engine room, a place of noise, heat, grease. Nick is thirty-five and gets paid twelve hundred dollars a month to keep the old tub running. He's been at sea since he was sixteen. Back home in the Philippines, he has four sons by two wives.

I ask him if he's been told what this voyage is all about.

He says, "Yeah, yeah, yeah," and goes back to tinkering with the engine.

He has a crew member deliver his instructions to the engine crew because his English is hit-and-miss.

The first mate has never been to sea.

We leave home waters without telling the harbormaster and without the required pilot in order to save money on the fees. We are lawless by nature. Because the ship was built for the stormy North Atlantic, many of the portholes cannot be opened. In the galley, this means cooking and eating in an oven. So the Captain takes a sledgehammer and knocks out a porthole.

On the way up the sound, we pause at Port Angeles. The Captain runs into David, an acquaintance, walking down the street with his wife. He turns to his wife and says, "I'm going."

And so he does.

On deck, Chicken Bob and I drink Black Velvet as the sun

hangs in the sky, refusing to go down. A pod of orcas suddenly spy-hops off the ship, all white and black, pacing us as we move up the sound to the open sea, top predators, killers of the first water arcing before our eyes. We fall silent and then finally the stars come on.

Below the water line the world is this: a deep rumble mixed with a chugging rumble, a faltering metallic sound as the engine gasps and works and gasps again and this machine sound meshes with the hiss and whisper of the water against the hull and this strange sound becomes essential to peace and quiet because when and if it ceases, we are dead in the water. And given where we are going and what we are going to do, being dead in the water is fatal.

From the quarters next to my own cell, I can hear voices arguing, a muffled yet heated discussion about the voyage and the chain of command and how we are going to sea as volunteers and no one save the Filipino engineer is paid and by God, no one is going to tell me what to do—that is what some of the voices say as we pull out of the mouth of the sound and leave land behind for weeks.

Captain Nemo said, "It isn't new continents the earth needs, but new men."

Four- to five-foot swells buffet the ship as we plunge westward.

Captain Nemo says, "Professor, I'm not what you would call a civilized man. I've broken with all of society for reasons which I alone can appreciate. I therefore don't obey its rules, and I advise you never to refer to them again in front of me."

Chicken Bob keeps thinking movie, that the early voyages against whalers, and this later voyage, are made for Hollywood. The Captain is his ideal lead—arrogant, media-hungry, stylish with his kamikaze headband. And always willing to die if the role calls for it.

There is a lot of that onboard.

The galley has four tables and a four-burner stove, framed by pale green walls. The Captain holds forth in a corner about Japanese crimes in World War II. The seas have gotten rougher, the room tilts as we eat chicken.

The Captain snorts. "What have the workers ever done for the environment?"

His table listens attentively.

He questions the value of nonviolence. Morality aside, what about the results?

There are really two types of crew members aboard. Those who know. And those who suspect.

We slip out into the fog of ocean. The seas grow heavy and soon a third of the crew vomits helplessly. The ship heaves and pitches. Aquagirl emerges from below covered with grime, her blond hair sticking out of her oil-smeared cap. She enters the empty galley, turns on a tape machine and dances alone as we slip and slide through swells.

A whale is sighted in the froth of the Pacific. The zone of the drift-net ships begins two hundred miles ahead of us. The fan goes out in the engine room and the crew buckles from the heat. I am sleeping twelve hours a day. My life has become a coma and I like this sensation. For hours I will lie below with the light off and feel the ship rock.

A grumbling slowly grows. Not for action, but for some clue as to what action means.

The first mate practices with the grappling hook topside as Chicken Bob and his cameraman record the action. Aquagirl watches, her face alert and blank.

Chicken Bob says, "Film is what it's about. In the early campaigns people would come onboard and object to the video crew getting in the way of the action. They'd seen film of earlier campaigns on television and thought what they'd seen was what it was about. They didn't understand that taping what they'd seen was what it was about."

We are all up in the Captain's room as he rolls the film of an old campaign. The Captain in his chair stares at the Captain on the screen. He mumbles a play-by-play as the action unfolds. Chicken Bob sits attentively as the Captain watches the Captain.

Chicken Bob says, "This is it. Solid McLuhan, media media media, the image feeding the image, whales as light as a strip of film."

A woman puts up an Edward Curtis print of an Oglala in the galley. She says, "I thought it belonged here."

The galley floor grows slick with oil tracked up from the engine room. We are a thousand miles from land and it is hardly a memory. There is nothing but gray sky, gray water, swells that look the same in all directions.

I'm talking with a guy on deck as waves wash over the ship. Twenty feet behind him is the locker. It holds three AK-47s, one .50 caliber machine gun, a thousand rounds of armor-piercing ammunition for the .50 caliber, ceramic body armor, and helmets.

There is also onboard a .25 caliber that one guy brought so he could kill Aquagirl's boyfriend, Big Indian, with a head shot. But Big Indian didn't make the trip.

Flour spills out on the galley floor, dishes break, cooking oil flows across the room. A man enters the mess, then goes airborne and sails across the galley, smashing his head on the hull. The television falls from its frame. The ship tilts forty-five degrees. We have entered a tropical storm. Of a crew of twenty-three, twenty vomit endlessly. The ship has no hot water, and in the arctic cold of the North Pacific, showers are impossible.

The next night the swells hit twenty feet, with some monsters topping the bridge. People fall down the ladders between decks and get stove-up. After three hours of drinking,

Chicken Bob goes and stands on the prow as the angry waters crash around him.

The engine temperature rises fifty degrees, the radio loses contact with the outside world, doors fly open and smash.

We cut power to cool the engine and so we bounce at the mercy of the big water. People tie themselves into their bunks.

I lie below and read *Moby-Dick* for three days while the guy in the next bunk vomits into a bucket. We begin seeing blips on the radar but we cannot move toward the drift-net fleet. The tropical storm holds us tight.

The hatches are now shut. Anyone on deck would be swept overboard. In a sea of about thirty-three degrees, they would have two or three minutes before their bodies would lock up from cold and sink beneath the waves. In a life vest, they would bob for a spell and then die from the cold. The ship at best cannot turn fast, and now in these seas with the engine failing, it cannot move at all.

We have no idea where we are in the Pacific.

There is a point somewhere between the summer of 1850 and the summer of 1851 when *Moby-Dick* begins to slip from Melville's orderly scheme and become the book that will eventually bring him back from the dead. No one knows when this shift occurred because no manuscripts exist that capture it. The *Pequod* sets sail with a ship's roll of thirty men, and by book's end they have swelled to a crew of forty-four, behind them numerous nameless souls. *Moby-Dick* is like a series of books, each emerging from the previous, and yet it is not some calculated statement of a thesis, nor is it Melville losing control of his material.

It is the writer coming into his own country, and he cannot recognize a thing but the ground feels sure and solid even though he realizes he's a thousand miles offshore on the deep blue sea and the captain is crazy and the whale lives beyond his comprehension but is absolutely sure to the touch. Suddenly things come and go and the going is unheralded. A character storms on deck and commands attention for pages and then vanishes and is never heard from again. The captain broods in his quarters and out there, out where no man can see, the whale comes, as regular as Kant making his morning walk to class and all those hausfraus setting their clocks by his daily passing, the whale comes on that annual migration that puts him in certain waters each year at a certain time, and by God, Ahab knows.

Melville, drowning in personal debt, sensing that his few minutes of notice are long past and he is sailing into personal oblivion—that Melville, sitting alone on the second floor of the farmhouse in the Berkshires with a view of Mount Greylock out his window and a blank page staring up at him from the table, well, he moves his pen faster than he can read and he has no time to adjust the tally of his characters, dust the furniture, press the doilies, or tie things up in those satisfying ribbons and bows that fit so snugly on the neck and, if you are patient, well, choke the life right out of you.

The whale moves, silent, running deep at times, moves, regular as the best clock and now he comes and Melville waits and wonders what in the hell happens next.

A whale spouts off the prow as the Soviet warship steams by our side. Our radios become useless from jamming. The crew of sailors mass on the stern and stare at our black ship flying a Jolly Roger. The Soviets have cannon fore and aft and the hull is packed with missiles sleeping in silos. When I was a boy graduating from high school, a local monsignor explained that each missile silo surrounding my city meant death for another city on the far side of the globe. Now I stare at the mirror image. We've stumbled on a picket ship, one stationed off the U.S. coast as part of a chess game now ending as the Soviet society disintegrates. They flash their lamp at us with a burst of questions but no one on our ship has the ability to answer.

The galley empties, everyone streams topside. After days at sea, the crew is hungry for any sight besides endless gray waves. Suddenly our radio works and a voice in English asks, "What is your quest?"

The Captain leaps into action with a stump speech about saving whales, the evils of drift nets, the death of the seas.

The Russians reply that they salute our noble cause.

And they tell us where we are in the Pacific, a little fact we've failed to determine on our own. They share their radar information with us and explain that there is nothing ahead for at least two hundred miles but scattered warships. They wish us luck. And then we plow ahead into the endless sea.

Aquagirl was born in California, then got married in Alaska and fished out of Dutch Harbor in the Aleutians for halibut and pollack. She and her husband would prowl the Bering Sea about two hundred miles offshore. Their permit was for two and a half weeks and the haul was normally twenty-eight thousand pounds. Aquagirl would fly to Seattle and then return with the cocaine strapped to her leg, the basic fuel of Bering Sea fishing. The past year or so has been Big Sur and quarter horses.

She says this softly, her voice languid, and her eyes glance at me now and then but mainly stare off into the sea. I'm on deck having a cigarette, she is on some route that takes her from a task completed to some toil yet to be done. She is never still and yet never hurried and she is almost always tilted slightly forward as if on an important errand. Even when she stops and talks to me, she gives the air of already being on her way somewhere. And there is always that faint smile on her face. She does not fit in with a crew of idealists and vegetarians.

"I guess," she almost whispers, "I want to pay back for some of the fish I took. Seems like a good cause."

And then she is off again.

Video cameras roam the ship ceaselessly. I cannot stare off into space without some busy lens capturing me. But no one ever seems to get a shot of Aquagirl. An almost feral instinct leads her to vanish just before a viewfinder eats the scene.

Heavy seas return. The ship seems full of ghosts, and no people. The boredom of the waters closes over us. The mess hall is almost always empty and when a few people do struggle in and try to eat, they sit alone and in silence. The crew do their tasks like robots and then hide in their rooms. What little talk there is is angry. The navigator can never figure out where we are. The Captain cannot find the drift-net fleet of more than a thousand ships.

A guy confronts the Captain in the hallway. Behind the Captain is a guy with a flare gun, ready to blow the confronter to pieces. The moment passes. But as the days slide by in the gray tossing seas, the moments come again and again. All that idealism needs to be fed and the food it craves is action, decisive, bold, satisfying action, and a low grumbling spreads throughout the ship.

A Canadian plane suddenly appears in the sky and some say it is tracking us. Fantasies of persecution grow. A rumor spreads that one crew member is actually a troll of the CIA. Another crew member permits no one else on the bridge when he pulls night watch, and this causes more talk. He also refuses to be filmed.

The Captain sits in his quarters rambling on about various environmental groups and how fake and gutless and greedy they are. His announcements have the feel of cold type. He says, "An alliance with loggers is a betrayal of redwoods."

Some of the women sit at his feet and look at him with adoration.

The handful of women onboard slowly become tension points. The males go about their tasks and watch and constantly wonder if they will be chosen. Nothing is said out loud, but it hangs in the damp air everywhere on the ship.

Then we hit a tropical storm called Winona and the vomiting increases. Two men sit in the galley and almost come to blows over whether voting is moral or immoral. Down below the water line in the dank rooms, the voices in the night grow louder. The Captain is almost never seen but remains in his cabin, working on a memoir.

The drift-net fleet remains hidden on the waters. Chicken Bob explains it this way: imagine you are trying to find fifteen hundred house trailers scattered about North America and you must search for them on a bicycle. The Captain asks him to throw the I Ching. Chicken Bob refuses.

That night a blip on our radar indicates a ship twelve miles ahead. But it turns out to be a freighter.

The Captain turns to me and wonders out loud if I can be trusted or if I will betray him and write harsh words.

Chicken Bob never rests, his voice never silent, a hand raking through his hair, eyes darting, a Buddhist who has no ease.

We are fifteen hundred miles from Hawaii and two and a half miles above the ocean floor. To the north through the gloom somewhere is Dutch Harbor. At midnight a fog rolls in and our wake becomes phosphorescent. On the bridge, the only light is the glow off the radar and compass.

The Captain sits in his chair and talks to the blackness.

He is climbing a cliff in Hawaii, volcanic rock, and his handhold breaks off. He grabs a shrub and finally comes to rest, marooned on a cliff. Then he sees a faint path and it leads to a waterfall with deep pools and the thunder of cascades.

He pauses in his tale, looks out into the endless blackness, and says, "This is as close as you get to being in outer space."

Down below, the Filipino engineer thinks we must use hexes and voodoo to find the fleet. At home, he finds they work well against enemies. And then he explains how if you eat shark fin soup, your cock will stay hard for a week.

His face is serene, he has for a moment escaped the prison of the engine room and the pointless quest of this strange voyage, and he is back in the islands and the women are soft and sweetly scented and he is hard forever.

Back home, he continues, men sometimes have little balls inserted under the skin on the shaft of their cocks, enabling them to excite a woman endlessly when they mount her.

Topside, two dolphins race off the bow wave.

The chill of the North Pacific has penetrated every foot of the ship and slowly the largely vegetarian crew has succumbed to flesh. Tonight, the cook, a committed vegan, fried fish and wore a gas mask to shelter him from this sin.

Aquagirl's cabin is above the water line, with a porthole that opens onto the deck. We drink white rum, she has brought gallons of the stuff. On the bookshelf are macrobiotic guides and next to them are various jars of powders to aid her in this diet. She is going to become clean, she tells me as she pours us another drink.

I sit on a hard chair, she sprawls on her bunk.

The ship pitches and rolls. We do not talk about the driftnet fleet. I think we have given up hope of finding them. Of course there is always the possibility of steaming into that Soviet harbor and sinking the rogue whalers. I have no passport and wonder if this will complicate my life when the Russians arrest me. The genius of our plan is we plot no escape. We simply enter the harbor, ram and sink and then, if we are still alive, it's off to Siberia for a spell.

This hardly matters as I drink rum with Aquagirl. There

is an unspoken thing that floats between Aquagirl and Chicken Bob and me, something we do not say: we don't care if we don't come back.

I have been to this zone before and I am tired of visiting it. I used to file stories on bad murders then go to suicide bars, places where men gather and drink and look for violence. I sat there for hours, a stranger drinking, and no one would try me, not a soul. It took me years to realize why: it is no fun beating or killing someone who does not care if he lives or dies.

The ship plows onward toward nothing. Each new wave looks just like the last, and the occasional albatross skimming the swells with giant wings only underscores the loneliness of the ship, a place of isolation where you can never be alone.

Aquagirl glances over at me and begins to speak. She is in the kitchen at home making soup. She is twenty years old that day and her father comes in and says something to her. She shouts, "Shut up or I'll throw this soup at you."

He keeps right on talking and she throws the whole pot.

The next morning she finds him cleaning up the mess in the kitchen, washing down the wall, and he says nothing.

She is seventeen years old on a visit to Europe. The drug deal goes bad.

She pulls a knife and says, "I'll kill you, motherfucker."

She is working as a maid in the Canary Islands and the local women bring things like casseroles from home and everyone eats together and Aquagirl likes that good feeling.

She is living at home with her boyfriend and her parents throw him out. So Aquagirl leaves with him and they drive off in his old van with two dogs. One night, they are cooking inside the van, fuel spills, the place becomes an inferno and her clothes catch fire.

She gets out, then goes back to rescue the dogs.

Next she is at a shelter, here her voice falters and she stares into her drink, the ship rolls and then rights itself, and she continues with her story.

She says, "I go right down to the bottom."

Her parents live only forty miles away but she does not contact them. The van is a ruin so each day she rides the bus. Her face is burned, her nose broken and other passengers avoid looking at her. For the first time in her life, she is ugly and she savors this sensation.

She keeps thinking, What would happen to me if I had no family? What if I were like a lot of people and had to make it on my own?

She decides to find out.

For a year she lives on the street. And here her story drops all details. She lives on the street, that is all.

She looks into my eyes. She has not done this before. The faint smile is gone. The rum keeps flowing. On her wall is a Van Gogh print, the wheat fields exploding with life.

I ask no questions.

She sips more of her drink and tells me that nothing shocks her, she has seen it all. Her face is without a blemish, the skin as smooth as a child's.

She says she should have been dead three or four times already.

It all goes back to a dream she had as a child. In that dream she dies violently. Since then, she has been waiting for her dream to come true.

"Nothing matters," she tells me in that soft voice.

She gets up from her bunk, goes to her sea chest, and pulls out a .357 revolver.

"You know," she says to me, and now that faint smile returns, "I've been reading these books about voyages and sailors and captains and in those books the captain always goes down with his ship."

I nod. I know where this is heading.

"When we find the fleet," she purrs at me, "if that Captain chokes, I'm gonna make him a real captain."

Then she puts the gun back in the sea chest.

She goes back to her bunk and spreads out sensuously, the mug of rum resting on her breasts.

We do not touch. We cannot get closer than this moment has taken us.

We continue drinking for hours in a warm silence as the night slides past and the ship struggles through heavy seas.

I crawl into my bunk. Chicken Bob sleeps, his cameraman stirs occasionally to vomit into the bucket he keeps near his pillow. Now and then the engine stops and we fall dead in the water and are tossed about by the swells. I turn on the small light over my head and open *Moby-Dick*.

I have fallen in love with Ahab because he has a reason for his acts and his life. It is not a reason that is ever made clear to my eyes—he tries to kill a whale and the whale in turn takes one of his legs. This seems more than fair to me.

The premise of the book is displayed but it is never made into simple sense.

"All that most maddens," Melville says, "and torments; all that stirs up the lees of things; all truth with malice in it; all that cracks the sinews and cakes the brain; all the subtle demonisms of life and thought; all evil, to crazy Ahab, were visibly personified, and made practically assailable in Moby Dick. He piled upon the whale's white hump the sum of all the general rage and hate felt by his whole race from Adam down; and then, as if his chest had been a mortar, he burst his hot heart's shell upon it."

We sail toward a drift-net fleet manned by souls who need to capture squid in order to make money. Once, they operated off Japan, but the devastation of the drift nets proved too great and so the fleet was forced into distant waters. It devoured the South Pacific in a few years and now it has come to these northern waters during the season when the neon squid flock here. Salmon are vanishing from long-fished streams in Alaska because entire nations of salmon have hit the nets and been erased from history.

We sail toward the drift-net fleet because we need footage, because we are bored with our lives, because we have ideals that life on shore mocks, because we once dreamed of a violent death, because the acid trips proved not enough, because we want fame, because we had a vision in a sweat lodge, because a magazine wishes a story. Because that girl turned us down and so we put out to sea.

But we have two legs and Ahab had one and he knew who took the missing one.

I go back to reading. Melville's words fly out like sea spray and there is no saving him or his book. He knows it as he looks out on Mount Greylock, all serene and lush and green. He will fail as a writer and his failure will be this: his only audience will appear after he is dead. His life will turn inward, fame will not come to his home, his family will dissolve around him. He will struggle with life until the end of his life and when he dies people will be surprised because they assumed he had perished decades before.

But the white whale and mad captain keep roving the seas. And no one has quite explained why.

One day the propeller becomes entangled in some floating net. One of the crew dons a wetsuit and scuba gear and goes over the side. He is down a few moments and then pops up and shouts to the rest of us the problem. He says it will take him some minutes to cut away the material.

And then he vanishes below the water again.

I smoke and stare out, I have given up pretty much on speech, save for a few quick words tossed off with Aqua-girl. I realize how much I dread the sea even though I seem incapable of seasickness and pass my time reading and making notes and savoring the emptiness of the ocean.

I remember as a boy seeing old footage from one of the big wars, the sailors forming ranks on the deck, the weighted corpse wrapped in canvas and sliding down a chute to hit the water with a splash and disappear. The moment always brought fear to my gorge. I saw the body slicing downward into some wet infinity, even though I knew the ocean had a floor and eventually the dead man would join it forever. When I got older I learned to dive, moray eels extruded out of rocks to examine my face, sharks swept past with open mouths as schools of fish vanished down their gullets, I came close enough to whales to spit in their giant eyes. None of this disturbed me, but still I dread the sea. In my mind and heart, no one can come to rest there. The ocean is too big, too alien, featureless.

The minutes keep ticking away. The diver stays out of view.

People look at the spot where he went under but no one says the obvious: Is he okay?

Finally he pops up, swims frantically to the ship, clutches the ladder we have dangled and just clings there, mask lifted, mouthpiece spat out. He removes his flippers and slowly clambers up.

His face is nothing but fear.

He got caught in the tangle and struggled and finally cut himself free. He had a full tank, ample air, people topside monitoring his dive, a good knife.

But the fear took hold.

He will not speak of it. He hardly speaks at all for a day.

The propeller is free now, we steam forward.

The deep, right off the side, the place we all will go should something rip this shell of metal that shields us.

The sea is dying and yet it rarely strikes back.

When the Atlantic sperm whales had been slaughtered, it was around the Horn and into the endless Pacific. In 1820 the whaler *Essex* was about three thousand miles off South America murdering whales with a crew of twenty-one, mainly men of the small island of Nantucket. They were out in boats chasing whales when an eighty-ton sperm hit the ship. The blow stunned the whale, it surfaced by the ship's side in a daze and idled there for a spell. Then the energy flowed back into its huge body, it turned and swam hundreds of yards out, then turned again and roared toward the *Essex* at six knots, splintering it. In minutes the *Essex* sank below the waves. The whale swam away.

The crew got off in the harpooning boats. They avoided nearby islands, fearing cannibals. When four months later they made landfall in South America, twelve had survived and the others had been eaten. The first meals died naturally. Then came the drawing of lots.

Melville during his time on a whaler met a man whose father had survived and written a book on the matter. He devoured the text.

A whale called Mocha attacked ships off Chile for years. Some say he did this a hundred times. Some say he took the pursuit boats with harpooners to the bottom. He was said to have been finally killed in the 1850s with a hundred old harpoon wounds found in his hide. He was said to be as white as wool.

That is all we know. Maybe there were other attacks that left no survivors and are storied only among whales making their clicks and singing their songs as they cruise the vast Pacific.

Of course, there is Jonah. A wisp of a tale from 1863 features a man going overboard from a whaling boat, catching his legs in the teeth of the beast, and being rescued after the whale was killed. In 1891 the *Star of the East* hunted off the Falkland Islands. When a whale slapped its tail, a man went over the side of one of the boats. Later the whale was killed, and as the blubber cutting advanced, the missing seaman was found inside. His skin was bleached from the gastric juices but he was alive, although he is said to have been quite crazy for two weeks. When he finally came around, he explained that the air in the belly of a whale was fine, but the heat was quite oppressive.

Or maybe this never happened at all.

The records are scant. It is clear that whales do not attack and kill us often. The squids seem defenseless as they gorge and fuck and the drift nets silently wait to kill them.

The ship plows on into the darkness of the sea night. We have hunted in our rust bucket, prowled the waters like a starving great white shark, almost killed our own kind, gotten drunk on rum, spun tales into the gloom of the darkness, and we are unsatisfied, our blood lust needs feeding.

In *Moby-Dick,* a black cabin boy named Pip panics as the whaleboat is towed through the sea, the harpoon buried deep in the blubber, the rope fast. He leaps into the ocean, becomes ensnared in the rope, and with reluctance, the mate cuts the whale free to save the boy. He is warned that if this occurs again he will be left to his watery fate.

The hunt resumes, a second whale harpooned, the panic returns to the boy and he jumps. He is left to drown in the immensity of the ocean.

Later, by accident, the whalers find him bobbing and pull him aboard.

He is never quite right again and even Ahab cuts him some slack as he jibbers and jabbers away on the *Pequod.*

Five or six blips show up on our radar somewhere ahead. Aquagirl is at the wheel. We are sixty miles off course and have basically blundered into the midst of our prey. Chicken Bob is convinced this proves karma.

We are approaching a line, and crossing that line means

being willing to die for another species. We creep forward and wait. We must be patient. The sun will go down soon and we cannot attack a ship after dark because the cameras will not get good footage.

The *Ryoun Maru No. 6* is out of Japan. There are a few men on deck in blue slickers, men who have been at sea for a long time working like beasts in a floating squid-killing factory. One of them waves to us with a yellow-gloved hand. The net is being let out and about every mile on this set there is a buoy and a radio beacon.

The captain of the *Ryoun* comes on the radio and asks, "What are you doing? We're working." He explains he is in the process of putting out ten more miles of drift net.

Nearby is the *Shunyo Maru No. 8*. Then we see four more.

We cut the stern of one ship by five or six feet and come to rest nearby. The sun finally sinks. We are black, the ship, the crew in black T-shirts and black jackets, the black flag, and on the side of the bridge in huge type ENVIRONMENTAL EXTREMIST.

Aquagirl comes by where I am sitting on the deck and says, "This ain't no real ship, this is a fucking love boat."

Chicken Bob is topside, face electric as he takes in the lights on the drift-net vessels.

He says, "I saw this graffiti in L.A. that ran, 'Death's the biggest kick of all, that's why they save it till last.'"

Aquagirl says, "The Captain's an asshole, all captains are assholes."

We have reached the point where we feel the need to say things because there is really nothing to say. The fleet is before our eyes and we must attack or be nothing at all. The ship floods with excitement and apprehension. The Japanese fleet is brightly lit, it looks like a Coney Island. The men in blue slickers keep toiling, the various decks glow, men gather at tables in the mess hall.

The Japanese men cut neon squid from the net under

bright white lights as the night wears away in the North Pacific. The sea is calm now, the loudest sound the forty miles of net screaming past the power blocks of the *Shunyo Maru No. 8.* There are seven hundred Japanese, Korean, and Taiwanese vessels toiling in these waters, or there are twelve hundred, or there are seventeen hundred. Nobody seems to know. Below on my bunk I've got a fat pile of government studies stuffed with charts and statistics, the kind of documents that talk about harvesting life instead of killing it, the literature that insists we can manage the planet if we'll just listen to the experts. The experts can't agree on the number of ships out here, or the amount of life left in the sea.

As an old captain explained it to me over a couple of pitchers of beer in Seattle, "Out there you can do anything you like. So don't worry about any laws."

The off-white vessels on our starboard hold men who do worry. The crews work like beasts killing beasts, tearing slimy squid from nets out here from May through October, the nets going down at dusk and up toward dawn, each net thirty or forty miles long, thirty-five thousand miles of nets each night, two million miles of net each season. Out here the numbers vanish and there is color and form, vistas of men at work under the bright white light, a light with the bewitching quality of Edward Hopper's paintings, a clean, well-lit place like Hemingway's café. Their engine rooms are clean, I think, and they do not break down. On the counter of the galley in one ship I can see a rice maker bubbling away, a spume of soft steam rising.

I sit on the deck the entire night, hypnotized by the vision of my species performing at the top of its game. We are so very good at what we do when we set our minds to it. In the twelve hundred miles we have traveled for this collision of ideas, we have seen four dolphins, the nets work so very well. I am drawn to the dedication of my own species, the willingness to live on ships for months, eat bad food, become a cog in a huge killing machine, forgo the faces of our children, the bodies of our women, the feel of home.

I am afraid. Maybe it is the old fear of becoming a corpse and then falling two and a half miles down to finally rest on the ocean floor. I cannot put my finger on my fear but surely it has to do with a sense of personal obliteration. I cling to my anger but my anger comes and goes. The squid feed and then the nets take them and the Japanese men rip them from the nets so that they may feed.

Dawn seeps across the sky. The lights on the drift-net fleet wink off one by one.

Then an order comes down from the bridge: "Prepare to ram in fifteen minutes."

The ballistic body armor and Kevlar helmets come out of storage.

The sea is calm, as if resting after a hard night's work.

Ahab paces the quarterdeck hour after hour while the crew watches and pretends not to watch. For critics, this is the pivot point of the novel, the place where Melville announces his grand intention, signals that this is not a normal voyage and the book not another sailor's yarn. Through Ahab, he slips the moorings of conventional fiction and in that moment dooms his career, his income, the *Pequod*, Ahab, and all but one of the crew.

The captain admits that Moby-Dick took his leg, he nails a gold piece to the mast for the first man to spot the beast.

Then he rolls into a torrent of words that mesmerize his crew and sign them on to death. He tells them the whale is evil and yet beyond his comprehension. He reviews the whale's quirks—he spouts heavily, he wriggles his flukes distinctively, old harpoons twirl from his hide.

He says, "That inscrutable thing is chiefly what I hate;

and be the white whale agent, or be the white whale principal, I will wreak that hate upon him. Talk not to me of blasphemy, man; I'd strike the sun if it insulted me."

Scientists now think sperm whales may have a motive for ramming. It is speculated that in the wild the males butt heads in a competition for females and that whales with larger domed foreheads would tend to win and thus breed and produce yet more whales with massive heads that can endure ramming. The scientists wonder if the ramming whales simply transferred natural behavior to a new target.

Ahab declares, "Forehead to forehead I meet thee, this third time, Moby Dick!"

But this does not explain why a bull sperm whale would attack a whaling ship. The males live alone. From time to time they wander into a pod of females with calves and possibly mate, but these visits are thought to last only a few hours and seem insufficient to create a desire or duty to protect the females and the young.

Like Ahab standing on his quarterdeck, we can only wonder at a whale's motives.

Chicken Bob has a simple plan. Pick one of the Japanese ships, ram it hard three times and sink it.

We have crossed some kind of line. We no longer talk of protecting anything.

Aquagirl comes softly up the ladder to the bridge, a bulky coat shrouding her firm body. She gives a faint smile, turns aside, and lets slip the front of her coat so that just for an instant I glimpse the .357 magnum stuffed in her waist. She carries binoculars and stations herself next to the Captain, who has commandeered the wheel.

The *Shunyo Maru* rocks in our sights. Aquagirl stares through her binoculars and in that soft voice relays what she is seeing to the Captain.

The Captain yanks a handle and the whistle screams and screams and screams. We steam toward the ship. The men on the deck keep working. We draw closer and closer and still they work, knives flashing in the morning light, and then the black ship is too near, the velocity too great, and something registers in the men cutting squid and they scurry across the deck to safety.

Our ship gives a shudder as we hit the *Shunyo* right where the capstan reels in the drift net. Just at the moment of impact, a big shark comes up in the net, gleams before our eyes, and then our prow grinds it into gore. Sparks fly, smoke billows, the big power blocks that haul in the nets lift up and fly away like mushrooms, the boom breaks, the side of the ship caves in. For a few seconds everything is frozen, we seem locked together, and then our ship slides off and returns to the sea. Cameras whir and click. The drift net, severed, falls into the sea.

Chicken Bob is on the side deck and his face is joy. A Japanese seaman opposite, standing right where we sliced his ship and destroyed his net, throws his knife at my head. It arcs through the calm of the Pacific morning and I think I would throw that knife also. I shift aside and it passes by my head and bounces off the wall behind me.

Chicken Bob gloats over his footage. We put out the Zodiac with scrap iron to sink the severed nets now bobbing in the swells. The fleet continues its business as if unable to absorb what we are doing. At one point a Japanese captain comes over the radio. He is puzzled, he says, he thought environmentalists were peaceful. We tell him we are not like that. Now we can hear many voices as the ships alert one another to the bizarre predator in their midst. This is why we have brought the AKs and the .50 caliber machine gun and wrapped our ship with razor wire. We pursue the fleet but our ship is a half knot slower and they skitter away before us. Chicken Bob dons body armor and a helmet and has himself tied to the prow.

The Captain idles in the water, playing dead and hoping this will entice someone to seek revenge.

Off our stern, a ship creeps closer and closer. Suddenly the Captain brings us up to full power, we wheel and go after the drift-net ship.

Aquagirl says to me in that soft voice, "He turned too soon, he should have let them get closer. He turned too soon."

We are too slow. We try the same ploy with another ship and fail again. Up in the bow, two welders examine the hole made by the ramming, as if a cannonball sailed through. One of them is agitated. He signed on for the voyage because he loves life, believes in peace.

The other offers that sometimes you have to strike back as an act of defense. As they close the wound in the bow they fall to arguing.

The rest of the day is a blur of bobbing in the water, the engine dead again, then power coming up and a chase. We pursue for seven hours before admitting failure. The fleet vanishes from our lives and we have hardly scratched its capacity to feed humans, to employ humans, to murder the sea.

Deep in the hold that night we watch the footage and time the impacts: 56 seconds total. The Captain stands at the wheel, barking replies to the Japanese ships as he steams toward them. I am behind him, my face a blank, notebook and pen in hand. Aquagirl stands erect, lens to her eyes, almost inaudible reports falling from her lips as we close.

Down in the galley, someone was baking cookies. Three of the crew slept through the rammings. The voyage has consumed $300,000.

That afternoon we radio out an announcement for the wire services. Our mission is accomplished and we have the footage to prove it.

Night falls, we send two men out in the Zodiac again. In the darkness I can see the underwater light as they search the seas for the second drift net. They find nothing. Somewhere out there we have liberated a curtain of death and it will kill and kill and no one will get the squid.

In Tokyo, officials deny the rammings. The voyage is over, the film is in the can, the crew hungers for shore. We become a blip on the screen of international media.

The thing fell dead from the press. In London, they refused Melville's last-moment title, *Moby-Dick*, and insisted on calling it *The Whale*. They tossed out the Epilogue, where Ishmael, the sole survivor, explains how he came to be spared a grave in the deep. And they took the herd of quotes on whales with which Melville introduces the book, strong drink that announces what kind of water one has entered, and slapped them on the back.

A person needs to know "And God created great whales" (Genesis).

A person needs to know "He visited this country also with a view of catching horse-whales, which had bones of very great value for their teeth, of which he brought some to the king. The best whales were catched in his own country; of which some were forty-eight, some fifty yards long. He said that he was one of six who had killed sixty in two days." Octher's record, straight from the mouth of King Alfred around A.D. 890.

And I need to know the word of Isaiah: "In that day, the LORD with his sore and great and strong sword shall punish the piercing serpent, even Leviathan that crooked serpent; and he shall slay the dragon that is in the sea."

Melville had tired of correcting proofs, so the book entered the world studded with typos and inconsistent names and all manner of piddling errors. The author believed they would one day amuse scholars and he guessed right. A cottage industry arose in the twentieth century to try to cleanse the text.

Melville wrote to his friend Nathaniel Hawthorne, "I have written a wicked book, and feel spotless as the lamb."

He would earn in the United States $556.36 for his massive whale tale.

His next book, *Pierre: or, The Ambiguities,* did not do that well. It has over time found readers but no lovers. It is a kind of car wreck other writers examine so that they will remember to use their seat belts.

The New York *Day Book* posted a review under a headline that shouted HERMAN MELVILLE CRAZY.

Aquagirl has gallons of white rum. She is serene. The day does not seem to have excited her. The ships were ships, their positions exact. And the Captain turned too soon, period.

Her hands are hard from work but her skin magically smooth and fresh.

She is not girlish and yet she seems to have no age, that gift some people have of being battered but never coarsened. She has put the gun away and we do not speak of it.

I have always thought that you cannot understand *Moby-Dick* unless you realize that the whale is truly a whale who cruises the Pacific on a regular yearly schedule. The moment Ahab fills him to his spout with evil, Ahab ceases to have a prayer of understanding the whale. The whale cannot be evil. He can be beyond evil, floating in a world so different from our own that no fall is possible and no evil can intrude. He cannot be superior or lesser.

Even with the rain and cold drifting in, Aquagirl has the porthole open and the air washes across me. Somewhere out there in the night sea a sperm whale swims, oblivious of our rusty tub just as, drinks in hand, we know nothing of him and his journey.

Chicken Bob enters the cabin and his eyes, always quick, devour the space. He takes in Aquagirl's cabin like a detective solving a case.

He's on a roll, talking a streak about his global wanderings, those big joints he inhaled in the Bahamas, the time he went to Thailand for a sandwich, two girls plus him in the middle.

Aquagirl listens, that faint smile on her face. We are all up and at the same time down. The rammings still excite. But they are not enough and so we keep drinking rum.

Aquagirl reprises her life for Chicken Bob, the thrown soup, the burned face, the street. She enriches the tale this time, how her boyfriend dumped her after she was burned, how after that year on the street she cracked and went to a pay phone and called her family, who came and rescued her. There is a car accident as well, and a settlement and the return of the boyfriend. Now, she confides, as the ship rocks its way through the ocean, she is down to her last fifty bucks.

Bob counters with the time he swam in the ocean with a female dolphin in heat and she swam over and put his cock in her mouth, and the time he put his head between the jaws of an orca. The time he looked into the eye of a whale and saw an armless Buddha. And now, he is sure, his life, his adventures, will be a movie, the deal is in the works, and Chicken Bob fills the small cabin with energy, he cackles and smiles and waves his hands and his eyes flame out and all around the room swim whales and hot dolphins and orcas.

There was the day he was walking around his farm with a gun in his hand, and he had decided. He brought the barrel up and paused because he thought he should wait just a moment, see if the world hurled him a message. Just then a 747 screamed overhead and he put the gun down and decided no, not yet, he would make one more voyage.

He says, "I came out here to die."

Aquagirl says very softly, "So did I."

I believe both of them.

Then she says even more softly, "I killed my husband, you know."

Chicken Bob stalls, a stunned look crosses his face. He is beaten and he knows it.

"It's easy," she purrs. "You know, just a little push, over the side. It happens all the time. Besides, he was an alcoholic. Everyone believed me."

Bob pours himself another drink. Then he reaches out and grabs the cords of the conversation and pulls them back to himself. He tells of his final days running the organization, his sense of fatigue, the emptiness that spread within him, this void he saw unfolding before his eyes, his dwindling pleasure in manipulating the media, in dominating others with magic chants, and in flooding millions of minds with brief seconds of calculated video.

"We thought," he says wearily, "if we could save the whales, just the whales . . . mind bombs . . . new slant on things . . . warriors . . . rainbows."

Aquagirl listens. Chicken Bob is very drunk and seems close to weeping. He says he does not want to live but his wife wants him to live, his children want him to live, and these people are making him live.

The Van Gogh with wheat fields glows behind Bob's head.

Aquagirl says, "I was lying, you know. I didn't kill him."

Chicken Bob's head snaps up, his eyes tighten.

He says, "You want me, you know you do," and lunges at her.

I can see panic and fear flare in her eyes as he piles on her. Her face says this is not a prank. I pull him off, shove him out of the cabin and start guiding him down the ladder to our bunkroom. He stumbles into his bunk and finally passes out.

Once, Chicken Bob wrote a story for a magazine that

posed a simple situation: Twenty people in a boat with harpoons approach a blue whale to kill it. The species is very rare, on its last legs. It is very big, the largest thing that has ever lived. What should you do?

Kill them all, he wrote.

He told me the piece got a lot of mail.

If we pick another species over our own, we become outlaws and must live beyond the pale and we are not likely to live long.

Moby-Dick would never pick another species over his own.

The sailers have gone over the horizon of our lives, gone over Jordan to their own promised land of endless squid and work and money and a woman in the port who will wash the salt from their skins and dreams. They have their own angers and loves and care not at all for our black ship and its hungers and needs and beliefs.

We have played out our hand and now must live with our seconds, those brief fifty-six seconds we will make much of for years, and the squid will swim in the seas and the nets swish down and the world will twirl, sun rise, and I'll think more often of Aquagirl's face drenched with fear than of the oceans dying around me.

I go back to her room. It is almost five A.M. She looks frail for the first time. I hold her and say, "He didn't mean it, he was drunk."

She cannot meet my eyes. She has been found out, like the time of the bad burning, she is skinless and naked and she does not like this feeling.

I joke about her tossing her husband overboard.

Aquagirl looks up and says, "You can't do that. Bodies float, wash up on beaches. It will not do. You need a crab trap.

You cut him up, cut the buoy, and it's gone to the bottom. No trace. It's easy."

I ask, "How do you get someone to volunteer to be cut up and tossed in a crab trap?"

She looks at me with bright eyes, that faint smile.

"I have a .357 magnum, you know. Would you like to see it?"

Red

Days later, under warmer skies, we plunge through schools of flying fish. Some land on the deck and we eat them. Each day there seem to be fewer words. Each day we get closer to Honolulu.

Chicken Bob continues filming. As the ship plows into warmer waters, clothes come off. Once, when the engine breaks down, Bob goes over the side and floats in the sea.

At dawn we are 260 miles out, by dusk 215 miles. The Captain sits on the bridge in shorts and stares at the sweep of the radar arm dribbling green.

The images are the key. Squids die, birds die, whales, dolphins, sharks and seals all die in the nets and this is of no consequence until it is seen on screens in bars and homes and airport lobbies.

Once upon a time, Chicken Bob tells me, if you could get vivid footage, material almost stage-managed—put young men and women in a small boat between a harpooner and a whale, put young men and women on the ice between seal pups and the men who club them to death—you could get on the few big networks and your bombs would explode inside millions of minds.

Now there is cable, dozens and dozens of channels, and no matter where your footage appears it is increasingly lost in the visual torrent. There is less time, film bites grow shorter and shorter, your script must grow tighter and tighter. And then there is the matter of novelty. Whales have worn out their welcome. Passive resistance looks dull. Nature looks slow.

He stops and falls oddly silent because we both sense where things are heading, that to keep the theater filled, the guns and ammo will have to come out of the ship's locker and even that will only buy a little time before the audience grows bored with this new twist, and before the seal clubbers, whalers, and the like begin to improvise and kill the young men and women who approach them with guns. We are evolving toward terrorism, the final theater game of the powerless.

One day in a swirl of fog pocked here and there by shafts of sunlight, we come upon a sailboat of no great size. The boat slowly circles, with a few sails up and tiller set to endlessly incise the ocean surface in a soft arc. No one answers our radio call.

As we approach, a man with a ragged beard comes on deck.

No, he has no radio.

No, he has no problem.

He has been in this position for three weeks, slowly making a small circle in the sea, and he intends to remain in this position until his dwindling food and water supply drive him to land.

He offers no explanation.

He asks for no news of the world.

He never smiles.

And then he goes below and we go on.

I feel a sympathy for the man, one that deepens later when I become a captive of that room and stare into the darkness dreaming of a negative of a corpse floating in the air just beyond the burning tip of my cigarette. I spent a lot of time getting to that room and even more time getting out of it. I feel a certain envy for the lone captain in his small sailboat who lives immune to our mind bombs and manipulations of images.

Nothing is in order here and most of it has spilled out backward, the cardinal's nest, the snakes, the room with a corpse, the elephants. The voyage that took place in some deep time within me, a time before which everything was simply a series of lessons and blows that drove me to sea, and after which everything was bringing back to land my tattered beliefs.

It was for me the moment when yes became more important than no.

The good times draw nigh and we must say yes.

The winter sun bleeds into my eyes, the trees yearn to bud, the birds—my God, such faith dwells within birds—are already building nests, and I struggle with something alien to my being, that thing the preachers and all the mothers have tried to drum into me: acceptance. But acceptance seems passive to me and I don't know how to be passive, nor do I wish to learn. I am a man of the garter belt, not the sensible shoes. And so I try to form that one short word in my mouth, yes. Black coffee lingers bitter on my tongue, and anger ebbs from my soul as I whisper it into the rising roar of the sun.

Yes, like midnight eyes.

I am tired of counting things, tired of mounting losses in my tally book. Everything I wished to avoid has come to pass. The world is very crowded, the woods and mountains and deserts and bayous marooned in the spread of people. The air has gone bad, the waters declined, the loins are now frightened—this I never saw coming, this fear in the loins.

I live on the line. When I was a boy the line was rock hard and neatly defined on maps as if inscribed by the hand of God. I wandered Mexico with my father then. I saw people living in shacks and wondered why they did not kill us and take what we had. Yet they stayed in place and the movement north was so slender a trickle no one paid it much mind.

One spring day in the early fifties in a Minnesota yard, a friend of my aunt and uncle came by, a big strapping man with a thin-hipped wife and a young blond child. He'd come back from Korea to a job with the sheriff, and now he announced his big plan: joining the Border Patrol and learning a smattering of Spanish and moving down to the Mexican line to guard the nation from something. It was as if he'd announced a move to Mars or the far side of the moon.

Yes to storms off the boiling seas.

I am living in the end of something and I know it regardless of the words told me by the authorities. Something that began with the death of Crazy Horse—or was it with the Mexican War? Or the extermination of the Pequot? Or with that early lurch up the Orinoco by Columbus when he sensed he was riding waters that flowed from Eden?

Yes to the mass movement of fellow humans busy violating borders and boundaries.

I once believed that a little learning could fix things, temper the lust for dwindling pools of oil, for the last forests, for the frightened schools of fish in the dying seas. I saw reason as a possible tool. I no longer do. I see the cards in my hand and like Mr. Wild Bill Hickok, know I hold a deadman's hand. And that is why I say yes. No has lost its value. The game is really over, that old game of management and dreams of empire and order and serene gluttony. Maybe it is the lap dancing that did it, the translation of simple randy lust into silicone tits, no touching!

Yes to nuclear weapons now escaped from the secret laboratories of the ancient powers.

Everyone is afraid of everyone else. The rich require huge armies. The poor yearn for small, cheap deadly weapons to protect them from the embrace of the rich. I believe in God

Almighty when I reflect that the first big bomb was fired at Trinity. Surely this could not be simple coincidence.

Yes to the crush of numbers as the billions spew forth more billions of souls.

The Mexicans are coming. The Mexicans are fleeing. And they are but a bubble riding on a boiling sea of change and movement. None of this can be understood by the authorities who live in the past where the word *no* had meaning.

Yes to the warming of the planet, the retreat of ice, the new burning rage of summer, the death caress of endless winters.

The ground seems in revolt but it is actually rejoining the fire. We have scraped holes in our sky and the rays pour in. We have clogged the skies with gases and the heat does not leave now. We are kissing the sun more fervently each day, surely we must embrace the rising inferno.

Yes to the drugs that police cannot stop and we cannot give up. The hit off the joint, the succor of the pill, the joy of the pipe, the grace imparted by the needle. The doctor will see us now and we will say yes, yes, yes.

Yes to the huge waves that will roar off the ocean deep, to the big winds that will rage across our coasts.

I have seen the hurricane and I am eager for the winds.

Yes to terror, which rises with the wind.

My people have turned to prayer beads, accountants, guns, and gates. We are many in number and the ground under our feet neither grows nor shrinks. We are in a land of dread and we know this and ignore this. We use words that are dead—global economy, resources, the environment, progress, freedom, capitalism, socialism, revolution. What we truly have are more mouths and dwindling food, more hungers and declining reserves of everything. And none of this can forestall the future. Nothing has ever forestalled the future. Something is ending, something is beginning, and this present cannot continue.

This is at least a beginning.

I've read that Beethoven ground precisely sixty beans of coffee each morning for one cup.

That is what I mean by yes.

I will walk in the valley of death and feel no fear.

Yes, I will.

Because of that one word.

Yes.

The Captain strides down the gangplank to the dock in Honolulu. Only one television crew has shown up for the press conference. The sun burns down, the air sags with humidity, and the Captain roars out the voyage, the mission, the action. We supply footage, those precious fifty-six seconds.

We are too late.

The event was days ago in some distant sea, the cycle of news is faster than we are. Our tactics are antique. Besides, the endlessly looping images of this thing called nature have replaced the need for the thing itself.

The Captain finishes and strides off into the city for some task. He will leave the ship now and fly back to the mainland. The ship itself will return to the West Coast with a skeleton crew. Eventually it will be beached in some cove in British Columbia and gutted. It is a used-up tool and it will be thrown away.

I walk back into the ship. For days I have thought of nothing but leaving it and now I hesitate to return to land.

Aquagirl has left her cabin door open. She looks up and smiles and beckons. I walk in.

She closes the door to her cabin. The porthole is open and on the deck bench beneath it a line of crew members sits talking. She takes off her clothes and so do I.

She tastes sweet and smells sweet. Soft sounds like lullabies come from her mouth. I crawl into the bunk and she climbs on top of me. The Van Gogh glows on that wall, the shelf of powders for her diet line up like soldiers.

We never speak.

When we dress and leave, the bench is still full of people. They stare at us.

And then we go down a gangplank and walk into Honolulu and find a bar.

Chicken Bob commands a table. We sit, Aquagirl still with that faint smile and soft voice, Bob a fast train of words about the voyage, the seas, the fate of the earth, the media. We drink for six hours.

I have entered some other life-form, some place that is comfortable and yet is not my life as I have known it. I am relaxed, I can sense her by my side, her scent floods my being. It is like the time I lived with the rattlesnake, separate but equal and not really separate at all. I do not feel alone and yet at the same time I do not feel that I really am anywhere.

At some point Aquagirl gets up and goes to a pay phone on the wall.

She calls her mother.

I am drunk when I return to the ship, where many of the crew are marooned by sheer lack of money.

I say, "Follow me, I'm going to get a decent hotel room and we can all shower."

They follow me like a band of gypsies, Aquagirl in tow. One by one they clean up. Aquagirl sits on the edge of the bed with a remote control in her hand and relentlessly plies through porn movies, abundant in this hotel because it caters to Japanese tourists. When I eventually check out, I discover she has surfed through over a hundred dollars' worth.

Eventually everyone leaves and we are left with the images on the screen. And then we go to bed.

It dribbles away.

I remember at some point she is behind me. I am sitting.

She puts a chokehold on me and I almost pass out. Then she relents and I turn and there is that faint smile.

She says, "I have decided on a new name. Call me Aquagirl."

And so, from that moment forward, I always have.

I fly out in a day or so and file a story for a magazine, a story without guns. Then I put my notebooks in a box and they stay there for many years until one day I look up in the yard and see cardinals building a nest.

In the dead city, months after the big water, I met a man in his sixties from Brazil. He'd had a professional career, then settled in New England, where the Portuguese fishing communities gave him comfort as he learned some English. After the big wind, he took his lunch wagon to the dead city. He sold pasta and coffee and soft drinks to the Mexicans and Central Americans who had flocked in for the demolition work.

He loved the women of New Orleans and the music, especially jazz. He'd taken over an abandoned house where he made all the food for his business, listened to music in the evening and had ladies over.

He parked his truck at an abandoned gas station in a district of ruins. The men gathered there as day laborers and waited for contracts. They would amble over and buy and he would joke with them. He kept all his money in a huge cup in plain view as he darted here and there, getting items, making change.

Business declined as the dead city sank to yet a new depth and workers moved on to dreams of better places with more work.

But the Brazilian man intended to stay.

"Why would I leave? I love the city. It has everything I wish for."

So he flourished on ground hundreds of thousands of people had given up on. He could not get closer to the future. I think of him from time to time. Of course, he is the kind of man generally seen as a fool.

We once were pretty sure we had killed all of them and eaten their meat and used their bones and hides. That was during the war called cold, a time when people talked of a winter called nuclear. We believed then in sudden and mass death, and so we thought that our people long ago, ten or twelve thousand years before today's breakfast, had made very fine spears and thrown them artfully and by this act had driven mammoths, those brothers and sisters of elephants, from the earth.

The bodies of the dead still show up in crumbling desert washes or the ice of Siberia. We have found corpses with the meat still edible. I like to think of them after their million-and-a-half-year run as going down under spears with their bellies full of flowers.

But now we may be cleared of the crime. Scientists are arguing among themselves about a new notion, that climate change drove the great beasts from this earth. The wind came up, the weather grew warm, the ice melted, and great herds that had dwelled for twenty million years were no more. Their size and might availed them not at all.

They were taken down by a world they neither created nor could influence. They ate, bred, loved, dreamed, and then the weather shifted, the ice moved, and their place at the table vanished. They live on in scratchings and daubs of paint made by our ancestors on bits of bone or the walls of caves. The Comanche believed the huge bones were from the Great Owl and so they ground the mammoth remains into a powder to treat their wounds and the vanished came back and healed and assumed the form of a new beast.

We will never be able to say the same of ourselves. We alter landscapes, we move rivers, we drink lakes dry, and we pitch our hungers into the sky and create a weather. If we go down, our hands will be on our own throats.

I have a dream, that all this talk of markets and cities and nations and alliances, all those long words and meetings of leaders are footprints in mud that will eventually be found like dinosaur tracks and create speculation about what beasts could have created such a thing. But meanwhile out there the last whale breaches and there is blood on the moon. And nothing being said in the summits and all the economic meetings or in the seminars and computer models of supply and demand, none of these have any more effect on maintaining the warrens of one species clustered in various cities than the prayers in the lonely churches of midnight. The real history and revolution is taking place all around us and is beneath notice.

Then I wake up and still live in the dream.

I sit in darkness before dawn, coffee steaming from the cup in my hand. The cardinals thrive, and both of the young are surviving. The heat stays on the land and the land burns. The storms at sea grow yet more savage.

The voyage, in a sense, worked. A few years after the rammings, the drift-net ships came under a moratorium because governments decided they killed in the North Pacific faster than the sea could breed life. But this is a detail in the decline of the seas. The fish perish, the big creatures flee into oblivion. The sky alters.

And I learn to say yes.

I eventually leave that room with the glowing digital clock and go into the gore of the city and find what I am looking for.

I live with a snake.

I trust the whale in the water ten feet away.

Aquagirl lives out part of her dream. Her husband is fishing off the Aleutians when he goes off the side and two crew members watch him lock up from the chill of the water, then slide beneath the waves and drown. She inherits his permit, a matter of a small fortune each and every year.

I devote time and money to saving ground and sometimes the effort works. My glass remains half full but it takes many, many glasses.

Sometimes in the hours before dawn as I sit with coffee in the darkness, I see that big shark coming up in the drift net, the skin glistening, and then we hit, and it becomes a smear of red.

I never learned if I would kill a fellow human to save the life of some other species. I only learned I would consider it. What I left behind was a preoccupation with my own species. I was trained in the world of men and women and children and their needs. When I came back from the ocean deep, I decided that their needs were too great.

I stopped trying to fix things. I moved into some other country where there were fewer problems. I ceased trying to figure out how to supply a growing and endless human appetite for flesh, metals, fuels, and weapons. I refused to be afraid of today or tomorrow or to dream lies about yesterday.

There is in my culture a fetish made of rules to live by and these rules are all about individual happiness and freedom from anxiety and want. They have little or nothing to say about other forms of life and thus have little or nothing to say about life itself. After Chicken Bob explained to me that the whales were armless Buddhas I began to see more Buddhas, especially in the rattlesnakes that increasingly were underfoot in my life. And these Buddhas did not care if I lived or died.

We have a wisdom literature about bending a knee to a higher power. I refuse to do this. We have a technical literature about conquering all forms of life and matter. I refuse to help in this task. We have a modern literature of therapies that promise personal happiness. I prefer the beasts.

None of these literatures will go to sea and witness the factory ships hauling up nets in the day and the night, especially the night when the world sleeps and men kill like robots on brightly lit decks.

I accept but do not submit.

The male cardinals attract mates by brilliant color. The scientists call this sexual dichromatism. The females look dull in comparison because flash could be fatal to a creature that must sit on a nest day after day. But in the culture of birds, flashing is life. Red-winged blackbirds flash that blaze of scarlet on their wings to other red-winged blackbirds.

Also, birds see more color than humans—we have three types of cones in our eyes for our dreams of the rainbow, they have four. Some species that seem one color to us—starlings, for example—are actually like Joseph with his brilliant coat to other birds, who can see the ultraviolet hues pulsing off the feathers.

The light comes on, the nest is empty now. The hatchlings slowly grew feathers, then tottered on the edge of the nest and flew off with the parents. They are dull at the moment, more like females than males. The parents still feed them. It will take weeks to make them sound enough for life.

And then they will go off and find territories and create more life. The males will grow a brilliant red. If they complain about this, I do not hear it or understand it.

I sip coffee.

I see red.

Lullaby

I know my daddy's rich and my mom is good-looking and
she's half buried by the tangle in the garden, there by that row
of pole beans, the leaves dark green, the pods hanging, but
the dirt, a humus that is rising from the clay of this ground,
that slick clay that puddles up the water and sucks the tires
down after the heavy rain, is buried now under a splotch of
black from the manure off the Holsteins, the tons shoveled
out of the henhouse, all this turned under, dark ground now,
the garden's an acre, the sun hot and the humidity without
mercy, and the spring seeps in, the summer comes, and then
the fall and everything grows and yearns and the rot adds
up and the clay disappears from view and the soil goes black,
ground my daddy says is richer than two feet up a bull's ass
and then he gets a quiet smile and bends over and fingers
the soil, and my momma's good-looking as she fills that pail
with fresh snap beans, the dirt rushes up, arrowheads come
out every spring with the turnover of the ground, tips sharp
and nicely napped, and you hear the bows long silent, hear
them in that instant as you bend like my momma over there
by the pole beans, and the next row is tomatoes, the leaves
rank, run the fingers and the aroma clogs the nose, the fruit
green and there, see the red one, pluck, take that up also to
the limestone house on the hill.

Fish are jumping, slap, hear that, jumping in the creek

down the hill, bursting out of the green water, gills sucking in the sweet air under the big willows leaning over the clean slate of wet, and then smack and they dive out of sight, jumping, going to do that until the end of time, and you don't know why and stare and learn the world's marvels before you know words or can form them in your mouth and sizzle, grease in the pan, black pan, seasoned iron, the meat hits and browns, supper is coming, the stove old iron also, wood-fed, and Grandma is bending over, but she ain't blood, just so old she's called Grandma, one of those ragged people come in from the cold and hunger and she bunks in the wooden addition tacked onto the stone house, keeps a shelf there with gallon jars full of salamanders and other strange creatures all floating forever in alcohol and on the same shelf the diaries where she scratches out the sunrise and moonset and how many eggs the hens laid and other details that manage to make a life into order.

The water comes from a pump by the sink and there is that other pump in the yard.

The outhouse has three holes.

The clay sticks and coats the skin after the rain and the air is rank with fragrance, scent, aroma, stench, suck it down and lap with the tongue, take it in and touch me. Touch me. My daddy's rich and my momma's good-looking and the stone on the house is rough-cut blocks, the stove is hot, men stand outside in navy uniforms for that photograph, a small print with scalloped edges and my God, these things cost a lot of money and there they are in a line all navy blue, Buck and Jim and Slasher and Bud and some are kin and some not but all are blood and the drinking is heavy and my daddy is rich and he's gone all the time and my momma's good-looking and she's cooking like a slave and men are drinking because they are all scared, that North Atlantic passage, an uncle on a drunk missed his ship out of New Orleans and it vanished without a trace out there.

The waters had long settled and calmed over the ship he missed as he spoke to me, and I could see his broad shoulders still shiver at the memory. When I was six or seven, he turned to me in a union hall and told me he'd kill me if I ever crossed a picket line. And my God, my momma's good-looking and she's bent over in the garden and the peppers are coming on strong, the carrots fat, the turnips a row of knobs in the black ground and the breeze is wheezing through the woodland to the south and no one at this moment can smell the stench off the refineries or the coking mills, the air is wet feathers as she plucks two hundred chickens a year for the table, the neck on the stump, swing of the hatchet, the hot water and wads of old newspapers, blood on the green grass and then one day she sees a weasel inching into the henhouse and stands on the back steps with a .22 and drops the beast with one shot and when she brings down the rifle the look in her eyes is of dread and disgust and the woodstove always seems warm, skins of animals on the floor as rugs and out the back door, across the garden, past the henhouse and the big barns, walking along the line of the woods and then the bluff and below is the plain with the river and down there, forgotten by everyone, is the line where the past still lurks in a dolomite prairie that came to feel the sun when the great ice retreated twelve or thirteen thousand years ago and the waters called Lake Chicago drained suddenly south and gouged and raced down new channels and began building with dirt the delta and bayous that became the bench for the creation of the dead city taken by the big wind one roaring day in the heat of August, there, in that nest of plants, a sole survivor almost for the region, a place left alone because those dolomite soils are no damn good for farming even though someone downhill and out there on the land created a functional steel plow in 1835 and the murder of the vast prairies began, but not here, the soil is too feeble and up on the bluff, the clay can be farmed but no one is ever happy with the results and so my daddy's rich and my momma's good-looking and I first feel the sun on my face in a place where the mammoth felt the temperatures begin to rise and its doom come on the warming breeze, and all this some thousands of years ago, and downriver the dirt piles up and up and New Orleans becomes a possibility as the ground under my feet erodes south in a fury of the melting ice and I'm a child and the world is solid, the house stone, cows lowing in the meadow by the creek, supper's on time, the woodstove never cools, the barns are huge and sweet hay smell in the air, the men on a Saturday afternoon sitting under the apple trees in the orchard on old wooden chairs and drinking quarts of cheap beer, rolling cigarettes and hashing out the last war and the next one and dancing around the fear and staying silent on the empty chairs for the friends who did not come back, and there's an elephant table in the house, a flat top and then a full-blown carved pachyderm below, solid mahogany, come back from Africa and I can't remember which uncle or cousin was ducking bullets there, ashtrays, solid brass and big from those cannon shells that the men cut down at sea as souvenirs and everything is old, real old, no one has had a dime for a long time because of times they all call hard and then, of course, came that war, and the rugs are not rugs but the skins of Holsteins that stopped being good milkers and went to meat and the floor, rugs of Holsteins with the hair on, all black and white splotches and when you crawl across them you smell the fields and life, and the men drink under the apple trees and my God, one day the fruit is getting ripe and the crows rip into it and one of my uncles steps off the porch and ropes a blackbird dead, hangs the corpse from a limb in the orchard and they stay away because, my uncle says with quiet respect, "They understand," and everything seems so solid, ain't never gonna end or change, and all the while beneath us are the layers of silt from that old Lake Chicago and the limestone from the silt of a forgotten sea and the mammoths whispering in the graves and saying, "Be sure to get a helpin' of flowers," and the Indians filing west to dust and dreams and leaving ground where they'd buried tens of generations and then the canals came and the factories and the stone house, carp jumping all the while, and the men stir slightly in their chairs and then settle back and don't care what comes next just so long as it is nothing like what has gone by and one uncle comes back and my God, he's been years in a tank rolling through North Africa, then Sicily, and then up that boot of Italy and it's real strange because during the hard times he walked off from his woman and his children in the Dakotas, couldn't feed himself much less them because the rains did not come, the clouds of dust rose like God over the plains, rose so high and mighty that on the coast they call east, the light got dim at noon, so he took off, joined that army, the war came without his permission and it was years in a tank, that tin can with guns, but still he'd gone up that land firing where the Italians live, tasted the food and probably other things I was not to know, tasted and come back alive with this new squash, zucchini, and it goes into the ground there by the limestone house and the meadow with cattle lowing and the world gets new and bigger and my daddy's rich, my mom is good-looking and she leans out the window of the house and says, "Dinner's on the table."

The old valley floor shelters purple meadow rue, old witch grass, big bluestem, raspberries, and feral plums, and over the rank green floats Hine's emerald dragonfly, and there is leafy prairie clover, there are egrets, kingfishers, and the stench of those refineries. I was born in a place so worthless the old world survived because the new world could find no way to work the land. I was born on the edge, the line where the ice stopped and then melted and the seas rose and the mastodon died out after twenty million years and the

mammoth, after a million and a half, gave up the ghost and
went where we all go in time. This is the line, here the ice
stopped, and before that, in the long gone, the seas washed
ashore here and the big house, where the woodstove glows
and the pies are on the windowsill cooling, is made of rough
limestone blocks carved from the dead of the long-gone sea,
and the ice melts, the valley is gouged, the rivers come out
of the ground, come out like the dead on resurrection morning and the soil of my birthplace heads south and forms the
place where all that jazz comes from and the refineries come
because of a big hole in the ground at Spindletop in Texas,
a gusher of oil that needs to be cleansed and then burned. I
can as a child at night see the flares in the refinery as they
burn off byproduct and the mills roar and the stacks shoot
black into my sky and that is how it starts, everything that
is my life, here on this line where the ocean left its dead and
the ice came and then the ice went and the mammoths were
no more, arrowheads coming out of the ground each spring
plowing, old tomahawk heads also, the smells never leave
me, and I spend my life living on this edge, the place where
an energy explosion comes into the world, one that changes
the face of life itself, first the rivers, then the canals, then
the railroads, then the oil and just across the valley that big
nuclear laboratory and everything is here, like surf crashing onto the coast, here all the messages of the big waters
can be touched in the limestone in a house made of bones
from a dead sea, and all I see is green and blue and the earth
floats as scent everywhere and the garden is one acre, the
fish jump, my daddy's rich, spends each weekend patching
holes in the inner tubes of the worn tires, fencing with sweat
running down his face, and then the train into the city and
the money and in all those scents I find a path as inevitable as
the mammoth becoming bones and then powders that heal
the wounds of our wars and the only song my rich daddy ever

sang to me was "Hard-Hearted Barbara Allen" and my God, the thing is blue and green, at first, yes, it is blue and green, because

> It was in the merry month of May
> When green buds they were swelling
> Sweet William came from the west country
> And he courted Barbara Allen

and then it goes well and then it goes bad and Sweet William sends his servant to fetch Barbara Allen and she sees him in his sickbed and says, "Young man, I think you're dying," and he turns his head to the wall and sees death and then to the graveyard he goes and

> Then lightly tripped she down the stairs
> She heard those church bells tolling
> And each bell seemed to say as it tolled
> Hard-hearted Barbara Allen

and so he sings it and the sweat runs down his face and the sky is blue, the world green and hush, little baby, don't you cry.

For some of us, everything begins with a lullaby.

> Rock-a-bye baby
> On the treetop
> When the wind blows
> The cradle will rock

and began rocking in the seventeenth century when someone walked off the *Mayflower* and met the Wampanoag Indians, then there was that Thanksgiving, the murder of turkeys, the magic of corn, and the tribe carried their babies in cradle boards and would hang them from trees when the women worked and so

> When the bough breaks
> The cradle will fall
> And down will come baby
> Cradle and all

and these songs never get out of your head and these feelings never go away and the cotton is always high and the living is easy and you believe no matter what mean street you are walking at the moment, once the melody starts, the voice purrs in your ear, you believe and at that moment, for a brief instant, you cease to be the fool that the world accepts.

The photographs tumble out, a pile of images with blood staring up at me, the old house, limestone in the sun, the creek, the barns, that first dog, the trailer in the woods where my uncle drinks and I run through the woods with his German shepherd, the boys back from the wars, the first big one, then that second big one, then some over in Asia, spiffy in their uniforms and whiskey eyes and cigarettes burning in their hands as they stare unsmiling at the camera and think of not ever thinking again, and the air is fresh, spring air, smoke curling up from their hands and down the hill the gas flares, the mills thunder, and by the ruins these shreds of original prairie survive because they are beneath notice, Jews hiding in some Berlin cellar waiting out a war, and there has never been a line that mattered, not between nature and whatever is not nature, between war and peace, between the lullaby and the steer slaughtered this morning, now the quarters hang on hooks in the barn, the flesh wrapped in cheesecloth, the meat cooling while flies buzz, the rough boards smeared with blood, and up in the house, the women frying the liver to go with the eggs and potatoes.

There has never been distance, just lullabies.

I float down a stream, bottle of wine in my hand, otters on their backs pacing the slender bow of the canoe, a storm slowly filling the sky overhead and I hit the marsh and glide among the wild rice and quack of ducks and one photograph is of my aunt on her eightieth birthday, she's got a cigarette in her hand and ignores the big cake and I know she wants it over so the poker game can begin and the whiskey come out and the next shot is of her farm, the bleak buildings making bold on the endless sweep of the plains and one of these mornings, yes, one of these mornings the song comes again and

Oh, do you remember Sweet Betsey from Pike
Who crossed the wide prairie with her lover Ike?
With two yoke of oxen, a big yellow dog,
A tall Shanghai rooster, and one spotted hog.
Hoodle dang, fol-de-dye do,
Hoodle dang, fol-de day

crossing out there, right behind the red barn on the lip of the endless plains, leaving for something better, believing, saying yes, and oh, Betsey is all yes, yes, yes

Out on the prairie one bright starry night,
They broke out the whiskey and Betsey got tight,
She sang and she shouted and danced o'er the plain,
And made a great show for the whole wagon train

and I can see my aunt's hand move in the still photograph, reach for that whiskey, start cutting the cards and the wind can howl, no matter, the game will go on till all hours and the future will be made plain as the cards are dealt and everyone knows the song, knows it in their bones and it has many names and places but still the song says

Oh Shenandoah! I long to hear you,
Way-aye, you rolling river
Across that wide and rolling river.
Away—we're bound away
'Cross th' wide Missouri!

Yes, we are, and the cotton is high and the fish are jumping, hear them? And the songs keep coming and I flip through the photographs, a century or more of blood slaps against my face and my daddy is rich, my momma good-looking.

You have no right to a better deal than a whale or a mammoth or that Hine's dragonfly, all but extinct, skittering over the tall grass in the shred of prairie down the hill from the big limestone house. Aquagirl is out there somewhere, the big ships with nets are killing, the snake is waiting by the path and listens for the footfall of a mouse, and the room awaits and can suck the life out of life, and the room is necessary but then, rise and leave and take Sweet Betsey and cross the wide Missouri, because one of these mornings you're going to rise up singing. Yes, you will.

In an ancient photograph my mother is eight, maybe nine, wears a rag of a dress, hair cropped short, and she is outside holding the reins to a team of horses hooked to a plow and her face has no smile as she rips the prairie apart and my momma's good-looking and there are long nights and they touch our lives and that is how we see the light.

And after ten hours of labor, the doctors said nature was not working out this time and then came the sterile void of the surgical theater, the whir of the saw, and suddenly my child in my arms and those tiny fingers. I counted them, a kind of inventory males do, and then he is swaddled in his mother's arms. I remember placing my little finger in his palm and feeling his hand curl around it.

We are always reaching out to touch a world we can neither fully trust nor flee. We see things but they do not seem to really exist until our fingers brush against the fur or the stone and confirm they are real. A friend taught drawing by having students feel a walnut in a brown paper bag and then make a sketch informed only by the sensations of their fingers. I spend a week down by the river blundering across sheets of limestone and shale, the bones of ancient times that form most of the ground there, and I keep rubbing my hands against the rock as much as looking at it. A desert flat never really exists for me until I walk through the brush and feel the thorns rake my legs.

One afternoon I walked into a slot canyon called the Devil's Garden and saw a sprig emerging from a crack in a boulder. I gently touched the tiny leaves and then rubbed my fingers against the brown rock. I was my son as a babe in arms curling his fingers around my finger.

Years ago, the morning my son was born, the body of a contract killer was found on the outskirts of my town. I spent months looking into the life of the man who wound up a corpse under a mesquite tree. He was twenty-seven, had killed fifty or sixty people. He began his murders at age thirteen in a Mexican border town. Locals told me he'd been abused as a child and they recalled seeing him fly through the air as he was tossed down the hill from his parents' hut. He wound up afraid of guns and did all his murders with a screwdriver or scissors. As my son struggled toward birth, the killer was being kidnapped in the parking lot of a shopping center and moved to his desert future just west of my town. That same evening, I stood out under the stars and gave a talk to nature lovers about a nearby mountain. I motioned with my hand and said that up there, in that darkness, a lion was padding by and watching us and knowing our scent and we lived ignorant of this other nation. Later, a biologist told me I'd had too much to drink.

The morning my son was born, I stopped by the grocery where my mother worked and told her she was a grandmother. She left her job and went to the hospital with my christening robe.

I returned to that same hospital about three years ago for the dying. My mother was nearing ninety and had a cardiac about dawn. They'd put her into the intensive care unit. Now the moment came to switch off the life support. My sister and I stood on each side of the bed as our mother slipped from coma to the place we call death. The lines etched in pink or green on the various machines slowly went flat.

We each held one of our mother's hands as she died. I kept slowly massaging her palm and gently squeezing her fingers. With my other hand I would from time to time caress her face.

I'll make it simple.

It is never safe.

It is always sensual.

We can see it with our eyes.

After we have tasted it with our mouths.

And after my son curled his tiny hand around my finger, I leaned down and sucked in his scent.

And after my mother's hand went limp in mine, I leaned down and kissed her face.

Gonna spread your wings, take to that sky, yes, feel the wind and rise up toward the stars, Melville's at his desk looking out the window at the mountain and his dreams are dying as he puts his dream on the page, the white whale is still in the ocean deep and so is Ahab, plowing the endless blue waters and staring with eyes of wonder at the dead oceans that they both now sound, and once for a commencement address I simply read from the long goodbye as Molly Bloom lies in her bed and wonders at the emptiness of life and the feel of life and why life is not simply her breast yearning and she says yes, yes, yes, and after I finished there was silence and then voices objecting to what the woman said and how she spoke of her body and I thought lullaby, remember those lullabies and you won't be afraid in the darkness of your lust and love and clean sheets, and I'm told it is hopeless, I'm told someone must suggest a fix, a solution, a way to avoid the way and yet the path is plain, been going down it hundreds of thousands of years, maybe more, no one has kept good notes, going down it, going over Jordan, going downriver, the silt riding and building that delta and then the city and all that music and gumbo of love and violence, the wind rises, the waters rush in, and I enter houses with mud and mold and no one comes here anymore and the feel is of a life gone wrong, of love betrayed and the mammoths come out of the ice with bellies full of flowers, and still, as my coffee cools, the cardinals build the nest under the blazing sky and I open a notebook and the words are in my father's hand, some slender leather-bound pad he carried in his vest, and his hand scratches out quotations he wants to keep and the first is by Martin Luther and says, "Who loves not women, wine, and song will live a fool his whole life long," and my daddy's rich and his hand writes down, "Far better to kiss the clay than curse the May," and he is gone with the mammoths and the little leather notebook that says it was patented in 1904, a time when the valley below was still lush, a time before the refineries came and flared flames in the night, and the seas teemed and I had not met Aquagirl and left port to die or find a reason to live, and I have no idea what people mean when they say hopeless.

My daddy's rich but he don't look good and I'm near the sky in the Shoshone Mountains, the snow comes in the night following a cold rain and I freeze in my bag while far away across the wide Missouri and other rivers, the man in that White House resigns and flees to the other coast where he sits and stares out at a dying ocean, and I come down from that night and call home and find the report is not good and begin to drive and drive and hit the Thunder Basin, a spill of grass and wind that rubs the horizon, antelope everywhere, and history has not happened, the antelope run sixty miles an hour and are chased by cheetahs that vanished from this ground ten thousand years ago when the mammoths left us after a feed of flowers, and finally I hit the desert floor and park, walk into the house, and my daddy's rich and sitting there at the table with a cold bottle of beer and we say nothing and then a week or so later they cut out the cancer and the long dying begins and now I read the notes he made as a young buck coming up, go through his old letters and my momma's good-looking and the beasts shuffle past into some mist and I cannot follow, no, I cannot follow but I mark the trail because I will be back and take it up and when he was dying my aunt came from the city now dead and they sat and her new man drank Jack Black, the old man rolled his cigarettes and she was working the river on a boat, gave me my first bite of okra on earth and none of this makes sense, leave the room and follow that trail into the mist, the one that crosses water and goes far out to sea where ships gather with huge nets and yet on the land, the cardinals pulse north and their young rise up singing and they spread their wings and take to the sky, follow that trail into the mist and find Sweet Betsey dancing drunk in the moonlight of the plains while wolves howl,

    and,

> Too-ra-loo-ra-loo-ral,
> Too-ra-loo-ra-li,
> Too-ra-loo-ra-loo-ral,
> Hush, now don't you cry!
> Too-ra-loo-ra-loo-ral,
> Too-ra-loo-ra-li,
> Too-ra-loo-ra-loo-ral,
> That's an Irish lullaby

because we cannot get it out of our minds, it scores us like a diamond on glass, and nothing can harm us, daddy and momma are standing by, and yes, that word, always yes, yes, yes, and I keep going back to the room and the negative floats in front of my eyes, the print dripping with chemicals and I stare and try to make out what happened and I know in my mind and heart that the negative does not exist, just as I know the boy was tortured, strangled, and dumped in the river and I will always know this and cannot deny this and so I will be in that room for a while and then leave, snuff out that cigarette, kick the bottle across the floor and hear it skitter and go, yes, go and find that negative that does not exist because the boy died and the mother is in tears and the facts must be honored even as they are erased, the mammoth shuffles off to doom with a bellyful of flowers and we miss the point, just as we miss the yes in her eyes.

Can I ask you a question?

Just what is it you don't understand?

Just what is it you need to know?

Just what is it you want?

I think the sea is endless. That's why I ran away to sea. After the storm—the vomit running down the deck, the bodies flying against the bulkhead—I lay in my bunk, the sweat pouring off me from the leaden tropics. I have a bottle, it is not my watch. I study the moisture beads on the metal walls, my body stripped and sweating. She enters and stands before me. The clothes begin to drop from her body. Her breasts stare at me, the hair between her legs, the long hank off her head. She smells very sweet, I do not know why. But she does. And she has no taste of salt.

"What would you like me to do?" she asks.

I'm on the desert flat and the buck antelope stands ten feet before me, his harem a short way off, and I am blocking him, his eyes dark and bulbous and burning into my face and as I move aside he goes off with his harem, ever watchful for the cheetah that has been missing for ten thousand years and I keep going through these boxes, an old letter falls out from 1918, my grandmother is in her twenty-eighth year, the honey crop failed because the clover failed, all the turkeys died out of spite, the letter says so, but the geese are fat and a success, and then it is 1919 and the Spanish influenza is killing everyone still and she dies, dies not even knowing what is stalking the land, this plague that did not come from Spain but erupted out of Kansas and she will be dead for over eighty years before the scientists determine it was really a bird flu, and my mother becomes a motherless child and is marked forever, but she hitches up the team, works the fields, and I hardly ever hear a breath of this, hardly a word but find it all in a box after my mother has rolled over Jordan, find another letter from her uncle who is over the ocean helping to smash the Germans for good and he writes my grandfather that it is God's will, and he writes that our death is set at our birth, and he writes that we can do nothing to change the date set for our dying but must submit to it because it is the way of the Lord, and I am close by the line, they are sleeping on the street or under the trees down by the river, and they tell me of their journey north, tell of the men who tried to kill them or rape them or rob them and they are rolling over Jordan as soon as night comes down but they are so very hungry and I start handing over money, ten dollars, twenty dollars, forty dollars and they stream toward stands selling tacos in the street, and there are many words for them and their fate, studies of migrations, failed economies, declining resources, words that clatter on the floor of a bar like small change, and I turn to leave and get into my car and they claw at the windows like animals and follow me as I plow down the rutted street and flee from what is everywhere but now is hot breath on my neck.

I'm over Jordan, I'm just going over home and the fish are jumping and the cotton is high. I was baptized in holy water in my mother's faith. I open an envelope and out tumbles a business card and on the back in my father's hand are explicit instructions that he is to be cremated and there is to be no service of any kind and none of any religious nature.

I did not obey him because death is for the living and my mother lived and so he had to endure the death she desired and my momma's good-looking.

I stare through the glass into the room as three doctors apply the paddles and then the surge of energy slams into her body and she is naked and right before my eyes she flops like a fish hauled onto the deck of a ship and they do it again and again and bring her back and my momma's good-looking and I say yes, put her on the machines and so hush little baby and I keep her alive for hours and hours so that others can gather round and then—did I tell you my momma's good-looking? The cotton's high, also—the machines go off and she fades away and finally it is summertime and the fish are jumping and I enjoy the warm nights and try not to forget and try not to remember that moment with the paddles in the antiseptic room.

I once was stunned by heat and sprawled in the desert and hallucinated a wall of ice studded with mammoths and dire wolves and saber-toothed tigers rolling past me in the midday sun, clawing at the land and reclaiming it and making it the way it was when they stormed across the grass and shattered the calm of the forest.

In the long ago, I decided to write this thing and it took much longer than I planned and became something I did not know at the beginning.

That morning she stood leaning against the doorjamb, bare-breasted, the hair black, the skin brown, nipples dark, and a smile riding easy on her face. Her teeth were very white and even. I turned away, I am always making this mistake, I turn away from the glow of that flesh. I turn away from myself, yes, that is it, from myself. I know it is fear, I am not a fool. How many women have there been? This is always asked. The trouble with this question is that it has an answer. And good questions do not have answers, they can barely break themselves into words. I noticed the faint mustache of dark hairs on her upper lip and wanted to lick them. There seems no end to it, and I have work to do. The aroma from the green coffee cup caressed my face and then I felt her hands on my shoulders, the fingers small but strong, her bare skin against me, and she said, "I'm crazy too." I could feel her smile grow huge then, and smell her, smell her good clean skin. She had just washed, her hair hung in clumps. Her clothes rode loose on her generous hips and it seemed as if they would fall at the faintest flick of a finger. I rolled a swig of coffee around on my tongue.

Going over Jordan and there is never a promised land because we are already in the land, the only land. Going over Jordan and then maybe we can face where we are and learn to be here and not flee at the first burn of dawn. Enter the mouth of the gigantic snake and in a day or maybe in weeks emerge, come out still walking east toward the light and have the new tools and songs and that food for the spirit, all this because we fear the snake and yet overcome this fear and enter the mouth. But, we are warned, not until we are ready. And yet I think we cannot wait much longer, no, it is time or time may run out for us.

There can't be a summing up, a set of commandments, a safe and sacred way. That is the path to ruin. There is appetite, there is the shift of things, the change in weather, the melting of the ice, the new rivers gouged, and the songs we make up to help us keep going.

And it is all words words words and she said that last night of her life, she was leaning back in the hospital bed, the voice frail, the face worn and tired of everything, she said, "I dreamed of your father last night," and then she let this hang in the clean air like a cigarette ring that is and then drifts away and never happened. And my father had been dead for over thirty years and she had made little mention of him for decades. Once, she told me out of the blue, "I never was afraid when your father was alive." And now she dreams as she enters the last night of her life and is on the edge of ninety, she dreams of my daddy who is rich and my mom is good-looking and I sit in the chair by the bed and know she is going over Jordan and why not since she actually believes in the river and believes in the other side and a part of her is happy because I think she always worried I'd get killed and then hell, she'd have two gone and be left alone in the fear and I'm going to see my father, so the old gospel song says, and going over Jordan and the whale's out there but so is the drift net and she dreams of my father and I know the dream is yes, I know the dream is past fear, I know she's got a bellyful of flowers and my momma's good-looking and the politics and the churches can't touch it, try to cover it up, they are things used to block the sun as it rises and shines down on this green ball of dirt and you'll spread your wings and nothing the priests or the holy men say can change this or explain the feel of flight and the sunless realms are in the rooms not in the life and so go go go, and I sit by the bed and finally she falls asleep.

And then come dawn, I get the frantic call and rush to the hospital and they are smacking down hard with those electric paddles and the machines come out so folk can gather and you'll take to the sky.

My father used to tell me this story when I was a boy about an old man who had wandered much in life and would come to the saloon in the small town where my daddy was raised and get drunk and then he'd dance all by himself and twirl and finally this dance would end with him kicking the red-hot potbelly stove. Each time, he'd ruin his foot and limp for days or weeks. And if you asked him why he did this dance and kicked that iron stove, he'd say, "You have to. It's *The Sea Wolf*."

Yes.

The smell comes off the woodstove, a pie is in the oven, apple with lots of cinnamon but tart, and a guinea hen out in the yard is inches from my sister and looks to be about to peck her eye out and my mother races to the porch and drops the bird with one round, and then that sadness floods her eyes. The breeze comes up, the sky blue, grass green, fish jumping in the creek and the garden is big and the snakes are here and the apple orchard fronts the farm and no one fears the offer.

The morning will come and then nothing can harm you, your daddy, he's rich, your mom is good-looking.

Hush, little baby, don't you cry.

Thanks

A few fragments of experiences in this book appeared in another form in magazines—*Details, Buzzworm, Mountain Gazette,* and *Wild Earth*—as I recall. But those scraps had little to do with this book and a lot to do with learning the things that went into this book. Also, I have benefited from the scholarship on Herman Melville, particularly Andrew Delbanco's biography and a book I read decades ago and no longer possess: John Bleibtreu's *The Parable of the Beast.* I should say something about music but I don't think we know how to say things about music. I wrote embraced by music, particularly George Gershwin's "Summertime," which exists in at least twenty-five hundred versions. I've read that Kurt Vonnegut wanted a single sentence on his headstone: THE ONLY PROOF HE NEEDED FOR THE EXISTENCE OF GOD WAS MUSIC. I don't know if he was right about the proof part, but I think it is as close to a proof as we are likely to get.

I also want to thank David Hardy and Harry Greene for putting up with my visits both to them and to the snakes. As for the voyage, it happened and I set the notes aside for fifteen years because I needed to cool down a bit and let things settle. The room, well, if you wonder about the room, you'd best leave home. The room will find you. *Sal si puedes.*

The Book That Is Three Books

More than ten years ago I wrote most of a book I never quite finished about a woman lost to the sands of Sonora in some long ago. In time, I took it up again and decided to write an introduction to the manuscript. That introduction got out of hand when it hit around three hundred pages, and so I set it aside and then, during one of the lean times that come and go in my life, I peddled it in New York as *Blood Orchid*. The same thing happened with *Blues for Cannibals*—meaning I wrote it on my own lookout when I could snatch the time from earning a living, and also when I finished it, I pitched it on a shelf. And then once more the lean times came and I peddled it in New York. This book has the same history. All three of these books—an accidental trilogy, I guess, though I find the word *trilogy* unappealing—are one continuous book and they all flow from a single question and a single hunger: How can a person live a moral life in a culture of death? And by death I do not mean something symbolic or metaphoric, I mean the actual death of other peoples and other living things. My life has been spent inside a culture of constant war and of vast slaughter of the beasts of the field and the grasses and forests of the land and of the fish in the sea and of the blue sky I was born under at the tail end of one of those wars. I am of that culture and yet I am against that culture. I am of my time and yet out of my time. I drive fast down freeways but I have no belief that these roads lead to a future. Nor do I fear or dread the future. But I do fear for my culture and the human beings within and the beasts and plants without it that suffer in silence.

This little project of mine got sidetracked by yet another project. I spent a lot of the past decade in the business world of drugs and I wrote three books about that, a kind of record of our deep hungers, our deep appetite for homicide, and our endless emptiness as we prowl the midnight streets looking for that thing we are certain will fix us. Or sometimes we search the noon hour as we doctor shop. But it is the same thing, licit and illicit, an industry of chemicals and hungers and dreams that never seem to be enough. In between these excursions into our lusts and little solutions, I worked on these three books.

I decided in answering this question to have little concern with publishers or the business of publishing. In good part because I could explain what I was doing only by writing it down. So I would sit in the midnight hour and work on this long thing I could not name or explain.

Some of the Dead Are Still Breathing is the end of the matter for me. The answer, as best I can see it or feel it or taste it or say it, is on the page.

There was this moment years ago, and I was living in a house without connection to electric lines or phone lines, sitting there on the porch in murderous heat, and that is when Beulah the rattlesnake entered my life. I'd just come out of Argentina, where I'd been camped for a week or two with the boys who had run all the camps where folks disappeared in one of those dirty wars. I got back to the ranch and everything was dust, the plants crunched under my feet, the grounds screamed for moisture, and the heat came on, one day was 117 degrees and I had no cooling, just that rattlesnake. The thing seemed to come out of that moment. Then,

I was in a burning world along the border and now, as it finishes for me, I am still in a burning world along that border. The snake—I can't say for certain—but she could well be still stirring, also.

When I started looking for the answer to my question, my world was sliding into what is now at least a ten-year drought. As I write these last words the rains have finally come—I am sitting outside with the light rumble of thunder and the first drops falling on our garden and dancing across the dark surface of my cup of coffee.

At my feet, a spent brown and yellow butterfly lies dead with its big wings open. The first breath of the storm comes, and the butterfly tumbles down the concrete path. I cannot name the species and at the same time I know the butterfly knew its name and it was not the one in the books.

Some people think the rains mean the drought is finally over.

I'm not so sure.

But as a desert man, I can only say yes to rain.

And I take it on faith that the butterfly laid eggs before it moved on over Jordan.

ABOUT THE AUTHOR

Author of many acclaimed books about the American Southwest and US-Mexico border issues, CHARLES BOWDEN (1945–2014) was a contributing editor for *GQ*, *Harper's*, *Esquire*, and *Mother Jones* and also wrote for the *New York Times Book Review*, *High Country News*, and *Aperture*. His honors included a PEN First Amendment Award, Lannan Literary Award for Nonfiction, and the Sidney Hillman Award for outstanding journalism that fosters social and economic justice.

ABOUT THE AUTHOR OF THE FOREWORD

SCOTT CARRIER is a writer, photographer, and radio producer. He was born, raised, and still lives in Salt Lake City, Utah. His print articles and photos have appeared in *Harper's*, *Esquire*, *GQ*, *Rolling Stone*, and *Mother Jones*. Carrier's radio stories have been broadcast by NPR's "All Things Considered" and "Day to Day," APM's "The Story," "Savvy Traveler," and "Hearing Voices from NPR," and PRI's "This American Life." Carrier was a winner of a 2006 Peabody Award for *Crossing Borders*, part of KUNM's "Hearing Voices" radio series. He is the author of *Prisoner of Zion: Mormons, Muslims, and Other Misadventures* and *Running After Antelope: Stories*.